THE CHURCHES
IN THE
NINETEENTH CENTURY

THE CHURCHES
IN THE
NINETEENTH CENTURY

Josef L. Altholz

Associate Professor of History
University of Minnesota

The Bobbs-Merrill Company, Inc.
Indianapolis • New York

Preface

A study of nineteenth-century church history in less than three hundred pages can be neither exhaustive nor definitive; at best, it can only be instructive. Such is the modest ambition of this work: a study of Christianity in the nineteenth century, written for the student of history, designed to be at once general and concise.

This book will follow three basic principles of organization: comprehensiveness, European emphasis, and historical relevance. Our subject is "churches," not "the Church," for the breakdown of religious unity is an inescapable fact of modern history which has not yet been overcome by a rising ecumenism. Therefore, our study must comprehend a wide range of religious bodies whose histories are not easily organized into a systematic pattern. Further, we must not confine our attention to ecclesiastical institutions but must rather examine a variety of aspects of religious life and thought in an age which was notable for great social change and the proliferation of ideologies. The sheer quantity and the extreme variety of the materials are perhaps the greatest obstacles to the understanding of modern religious history. For the purpose of this book, conciseness and coherence may best be achieved by a relative limitation of our view to the European heartland of Christendom. Therefore, although the expansion of Christianity outside Europe is a part of our story, it will take second place to the study of what happened in Europe itself, which was still the central core of the Christian world. This may appear strange in view of the fact that the nineteenth century has been called the "Great Century" of church history because of its significance in the expansion of Christianity from a European to a world religion. European history, however, has a unity of its own which ought not to be sacrificed to a "world history" whose trends we can still only faintly discern. The history of the Christian churches finds its place in the context of European history, and it deserves to be studied in that context. The question which is central to this study, and to which we shall constantly recur, is this: what was the relation of the churches to the new society which emerged in Europe in this revolutionary period?

Even more than in matters of organization, this book will differ from many other general works on modern church history in the spirit in which the author approaches his subject. The history of Christianity is a study usually undertaken by persons with definite denominational commitments, and their writings frequently reflect these commitments. What is needed is a study of church history which is neither Catholic nor Protestant, nor even distinctively Christian, but simply historical. As Cardinal Newman said, "Christianity has been long enough in the world to justify us in dealing with it as a fact in the world's history." It is as facts in the world's history, worthy of our disinterested curiosity, that we shall seek to study the Christian churches in nineteenth-century Europe.

This book was projected as part of a multi-volume "History of the Church" under the general editorship of Professor Robert S. Hoyt of the University of Minnesota, to whom I am indebted for much invaluable assistance. Great freedom was allowed to the authors, so that this volume reflects my own idiosyncrasies rather than any editorial policy. The writing of this book was made possible by a fellowship granted by the John S. Guggenheim Memorial Foundation for the academic year 1964–1965. I am indebted for much stimulating conversation and many helpful suggestions to several of my colleagues, particularly Professors Timothy Smith, Theofanis Stavrou, and Karl F. Morrison, now of the University of Chicago. The map illustrating Chapters six and seven was prepared by the Department of Geography of the University of Minnesota. Finally, I must express my appreciation for the patient listening of the students in my pro-seminar in modern European religious history.

JOSEF L. ALTHOLZ

Minneapolis, Minnesota
September 1966

CONTENTS

ix

THE CHURCHES
IN THE
NINETEENTH CENTURY

1

The Problem of Religion
in the Modern World

The Christian religion provided the matrix in which Western European civilization was formed. Under the aegis of the Roman Catholic Church, the peoples of Europe in the Middle Ages achieved a remarkable cultural synthesis, a harmony of religion and society never equalled in succeeding epochs. Even by the later Middle Ages, religion was losing its place as the focus of European life, with the development of the new secular interests of the humanistic Renaissance, capitalistic commerce, and the sovereign state. Once again religion came briefly to the center of the historical stage in that outburst of spiritual energy which produced the Protestant Reformation and the Roman Catholic Counter-Reformation; yet the result of the Reformations was but to confirm the disunity of Europe, with religion added to other grounds of discord. Europe had to come to terms with the fact of division along religious lines.

Perhaps as a reaction from these titanic struggles in the name of religion, the modern world turned itself with redoubled energy to the secular interests of commerce, the state, and the autonomous intellect. In the eighteenth century the religious monopoly of Christianity was challenged by those who held that religion had no need of churches or creeds; and there were those who asserted that man had no need of religion at all. At the end of this century of relatively feeble religious life came a Revolution which threatened to sweep away Christianity along with a host of other institutions now deemed outworn. Even when "order" was restored after the storm of revolution had passed, there were left behind revolutionary ideologies which challenged the Christian faith for the allegiance of men's minds in a society which no longer gave to the churches the support to which they had become accustomed.

Thus we come to the central problem of modern religious history: what was to be the role of Christianity in a society to which religion was increasingly alien? This problem was most acute in the nineteenth century, in which the Christian religion had to make its way amid a fluid social and political structure, an expanding economy and population, and competitive ideologies. Yet it is not enough to call the nineteenth century a revolutionary age: it was an age of new possibilities, in which, if there were challenges to faith, there were also opportunities for Christian development. The themes of crisis and revival parallel each other throughout the century, which ended with a paradoxical situation in which the churches were showing increasing vigor in a society in which religion was decreasingly a vital factor. It is this imperfect resolution of the religious problem which confronts us at present, for in the middle of the twentieth century we are still working out the consequences of the nineteenth.

From the standpoint of religious history, certain general characteristics of the nineteenth century should be noted. The first of these is the geographical expansion of Christendom. The expansion of Western civilization outside the confines of Europe, by exploration, conquest, and settlement, had begun in the fifteenth century; it had been accompanied by an expansion of the area of Christian influence. This process took a great leap forward in the nineteenth century. Whole continents hitherto relatively untouched became subject to European political, economic, and cultural influences. And at the same time as Europe was extending its external domination over alien cultures, the area of Western culture was being extended by the emigration and settlement of Europeans overseas. In both aspects of the expansion of Europe, the expansion of Christianity was a part of the process: through missions and migration it now became a world-wide religion, with greatly increased numbers. Christendom was outgrowing Europe, which, however, remained its heartland throughout the century.

The large-scale migration of Europeans overseas was only one aspect of the "population explosion" which characterized nineteenth-century Europe. The number of Europeans roughly tripled in the course of the century. This signified a vast increase in the number of nominal Christians: the Christian proportion of the world's population was larger than it has ever been before or since. On the other hand, the increased population was a mixed blessing to the churches, for established ecclesiastical institutions were not designed to serve such large numbers. The fact that these masses tended to congregate in new urban agglomerations presented further problems to churches which had originated in an agrarian society.

This change from an agrarian to an urban society, with its attendant progress and problems, represented a transformation of the material and social conditions of human life probably unprecedented in the history of civilization. The "Industrial Revolution" of the nineteenth century resulted, in its economic aspects, in a vast increase in the quantity of goods produced and in the scale of production; in its social aspects, it signified the removal of feudal survivals, the dominance of the middle classes, and the development of an urban proletariat—a class quite different from the agrarian "poor" which Christians had always had with them. To these new classes, with their essentially materialistic interests, the churches had to make new appeals; to the social problems resulting from economic change they had to find new Christian responses. The adjustment of the churches, themselves products of the old order, to the new society was made difficult by the revolutionary class struggles which accompanied the transformation of the economy. The temptation was always present to identify the cause of religion with the defense of the existing order. In the process a gulf tended to develop between the churches, still basically oriented toward an older society, and the new masses growing in numbers and strength.

The social revolution was related to the political situation with which the churches were confronted. The secular state, impersonal, bureaucratic, tending to control all aspects of social life, had since the Renaissance presented challenges to the independence and integrity of the churches. The nineteenth century saw the rise of new secular forces—bourgeois Liberalism, the radical democracy of the working classes, and nationalism—struggling for control of the political apparatus. The churches, usually finding themselves on the losing side, were among the leading victims of the revolutions of the age. The Church-State conflict progressed from the attempt to subordinate the church to the state to a more thorough anti-clericalism and, frequently, to an outright hostility to religion.

It is not sufficient, however, to consider the crisis of the churches in the modern age under the traditional heading of the relations of Church and State. The issues were now vaster: it was a question of Church and Society. All the various conflicts in which the churches were involved were merely aspects of the general process of secularization of European life which, beginning with the breakdown of the medieval synthesis, seemed to have reached its culmination in the nineteenth century.

This process of secularization is most evident in the sphere of the intellect, in which the transference of values from the divine to the human—from the eternal to the temporal—was explicit. The seventeenth and eighteenth centuries had produced a number of autonomous intellectual disciplines—the physical and social sciences—which allowed no place to the premises of faith. In the "Enlightenment" of the eighteenth century, a picture emerged of a material universe operating according to impersonal mathematical formulae and of a social and political order governed by natural laws, ascertainable by the human reason, and capable of being employed to produce a progressively better life for man. This purely natural world-picture, towards which the sciences were tending, left little room for religion; it seemed that European civilization in this materialistic age was outgrowing the Christianity which had formed it. Yet the values of the secular sciences were themselves products of the Christian heritage: intellectual truthfulness and social benevolence are also religious virtues. When a conflict, whether necessary or accidental, developed between the conclusions of the sciences and the accepted doctrines of the Christian religion, there resulted a crisis in the European conscience from the effects of which it has perhaps not yet recovered.

The geographical and population expansion of European civilization widened the field within which the Christian churches had to operate. The Industrial Revolution, the revolutionary political situation, and the revolutions in the intellectual sphere presented the churches with new problems both different from and greater than the still-unresolved problems of the past. In the nineteenth century, more than at any time since it had triumphed over ancient paganism, the Christian religion, divided within itself, was thrust into a competitive situation. The question was now, not whether Christianity would remain united or retain its traditional status, but whether it could survive at all amid the collapse of the old order. Christianity was challenged to prove, not merely its truth, but its relevance.

2

The Eighteenth-Century Background

Between the great ecclesiastical struggles of the sixteenth century and the religious revival of the nineteenth, the eighteenth century stands as a lull, a period of relatively feeble activity for the churches. We think of this century, perhaps with some exaggeration, as the "Age of Reason," the "Enlightenment," a period of high culture, intellectual progress, and political development —but not of great spirituality. The contrast is especially marked with the preceding epoch, the Reformation and Wars of Religion, when religious issues occupied a central place in the history of the times. Now, as once before in the Renaissance, the secular interests of man reasserted themselves. The shift of values was all the more profound for being undramatic: Christianity was not so much denied as relegated to the background.

The most significant sign of this religious indifference was one which, in other circumstances, might have been celebrated as a triumph of Christian love: the decline of religious persecution. The idea of toleration had been anathema in the age of the Reformation, when men's souls were regarded as being staked on fine points of doctrine. The separation of church and state was almost unknown, and each state maintained its established church, insisting upon religious unity as a civil as well as a religious necessity. Nonetheless, the fact, if not the principle, of religious diversity began to be recognized and allowed. Beginning with the admission that each state was free to choose the religion of its subjects—the formula *cuius regio, eius religio* (as the prince, so the religion)—some nations reached the point of recognizing that there were religious minorities within the state which were too strong to be either absorbed or eliminated. Further, this increasingly capitalistic age discovered that intolerance was commercially inconvenient: the most enterprising businessmen were frequently members of religious minorities, and one does not discuss differences of faith in the marketplace. Men soon grew weary of an unprofitable persecution.

The expulsion of the Huguenots from France by Louis XIV in 1685 was almost the last of the great persecutions, although an archbishop of Salzburg expelled his Protestants as late as 1731. It is significant that these acts aroused severe criticism, and not only among Protestants. Similarly the sporadic cases of individual persecution, notably the judicial murder of Calas in 1762, were all the more prominent because of their relative rarity and the indignation with which they were condemned by the leading intellectuals. Another striking sign of the new attitude was the decline of persecutions for witchcraft. This mania, which had reached epidemic proportions, was severely criticized by the end of the seventeenth century, and witch-burning gradually ceased. The abandonment of belief in witchcraft was not necessarily a sign of deeper religious insight, but rather of indifference: "The giving up of witchcraft," John Wesley lamented, "is in effect giving up the Bible."

Few states, however, were willing to give up the principle of religious unity. The most notable exceptions were the two most commercially successful nations, Holland and England. The Dutch, whose struggle for independence had been inspired by a militant Calvinism, found themselves with a large Catholic minority and with a group of dissidents—the anti-predestinarian Arminians—among the Protestants. They deemed it prudent, while supporting the Reformed Church, to extend toleration to others. Holland thus became the refuge of oppressed minorities from all over Europe: Separatists from England, Anabaptist sectaries from Germany, Huguenots from France, Jews from Spain and Portugal. England's road to toleration was more tortuous.

The "Church of England as by law established" had been designed to secure the peace of the kingdom by comprehending as much as possible of the diverse religious traditions, Catholic and Protestant; it became instead a battleground for contending factions. The Civil Wars (1642–1660) represented the attempt of the Calvinistic Puritans to capture the established church. They failed, and those who could not conform to Anglicanism had to form "dissenting" or "nonconforming" religious bodies. In the process, the Puritans discovered that they were not united among themselves, and they divided into separate Presbyterian, Congregational, and Baptist denominations. At the same time, the Anglican Church learned that it could hope neither to comprehend the full range of English religious sentiments nor to suppress those who would not conform. Grudgingly, toleration was extended to Protestant nonconformists; they were free to carry on their own religious life, although political power was monopolized by Anglicans. In the eighteenth century England was regarded as the home of civil and religious freedom. Along with Holland, it was a center from which radiated the new modes of thought which shaped the Age of the Enlightenment.

This age began with an intellectual revolution of a magnitude unprecedented in western history. The traditional cosmology, inherited from the ancients and sanctified by religion, was centered upon man as a spiritual being with a peculiar relation to an arbitrary God. These presuppositions were assailed by the scientific revolution of the seventeenth century which shifted men's interests from the supernatural to the natural order. The heliocentric astronomy of Copernicus, popularized and extended by Galileo, challenged the belief that the earth was the fixed center of the universe and came into apparent conflict with the literal text of the Bible. The new astronomy was verified by experiment, and the experimental or inductive method was proposed as the basis of a renovation of learning by Francis Bacon. The more rigorously logical Descartes proposed to organize the physical universe under the laws of mathematics. The scientific method could be applied to the mental as well as the physical universe: John Locke devised a psychology which regarded

thought as nothing more than the perception of external sensations, leaving no place for "innate ideas." This century of scientific progress culminated with Sir Isaac Newton, who combined
the experimental and mathematical methods and ascertained the
general laws of motion. The natural world was shown to be
governed by mathematical laws, discovered by the human mind
unaided by revelation. It was an intoxicating triumph of man's
intellect, summed up by Pope's couplet:

> Nature and Nature's Laws lay hid in night;
> God said "Let Newton be," and all was Light.

Nature was the object of man's study, reason the sole method,
and "light" the result: such were the themes of the "Enlightenment." This new vision of a mechanistic universe, governed by
impersonal nature laws, left little room for the traditional concerns of Christianity. The existence of God, indeed, was not immediately challenged, for it was necessary to explain the creation
of the universe and the institution of its laws; but the God thus
envisioned was exceedingly impersonal. He was referred to, even
in hymns, as the "Creator," the "First Cause," or "Providence";
some called him the "Great Watchmaker"; the Masons adored
the "Great Architect of the Universe." In this there is nothing of
the Jehovah of the Old Testament or the Savior of the New, nor
could the Fall and the Atonement have much meaning for those
who saw man as a free and noble being capable of perfecting
himself through his intellectual progress.

The new science exalted doubt and free inquiry. Notions of
unchallenged authority, uncritical faith, and unverified revelation were discredited as "superstitious." The new science of doc-
umentary history led to a critical examination of the Biblical
text. Pierre Bayle, whose *Historical and Critical Dictionary* was a
model for later skeptics, engaged in an internal criticism of the
Bible stories, finding them neither divinely inspired nor morally
elevating. Meanwhile travel books were telling Europeans about
non-Christian societies whose morality seemed to meet or surpass
the standards of Christendom, thus casting doubt on the moral

uniqueness of the Christian faith. The new attitude was above all critical; and criticism soon led to skepticism.

The churches could not let this challenge go without response; but the response was more disastrous than the challenge. Accustomed to command, not to debate, and ever fearful of opinions dangerous to faith, the churches met the intellectual challenge by invoking the principle of authority which was itself the subject of dispute. Because its apparatus for the detection and suppression of heresy was the most efficient, the Roman Catholic Church took the leading role in this struggle; it thus came to be regarded, more than any other church, as the citadel of bigotry, intolerance, and superstition. Copernican astronomy was condemned in 1616 as contrary to Scripture and philosophy, and Galileo was forced to recant in 1632. Descartes sought to avoid theological difficulties by a dualism which in effect asserted the mutual independence of science and religion; but this doctrine too was condemned. The condemnation of Copernicanism was reversed in 1757, but by then the damage had been done, and the conflict was irreconcilable. The policy of condemnation, censorship, and petty persecutions continued into the eighteenth century, redeemed only by its inefficiency. The maladroitness of the Church, far from crushing the new science, gave it a triumph greater than it deserved. An intellectual crisis ensued, as educated men had to choose between an orthodoxy defended by a discredited authority and a scientific outlook demonstrated by reason. They chose reason; and it took the churches a century to regain their intellectual respectability.

The victorious Enlightenment did not, however, dispense with religion. It devised a new religious position, "Deism," or "natural religion." Deism is the doctrine that there are certain simple universal truths fundamental to all religions, natural to man, evident to his reason, and sufficient for his spiritual needs. These truths are: the existence of God, who created the universe and instituted its laws; the propriety of worship and virtue; and a future life of rewards and punishments as the sanction of morality. The assertion of the universality of natural religion is an implicit denial of special revelation, so that Deism was ultimately non-Christian; yet it is the historical product of a Christian culture from which it drew many of its aspirations. In one sense Deism may be regarded as a new Reformation, an attempt to purify Christianity of abuses which had crept in during the course of history, and especially of abuses in the intellectual foundations of religion. But the abuses proved to be identical with the foundations. In stripping away tradition, authority, prophecy, miracles, and mystery, the Deists stripped away everything that was characteristically Christian in Christianity; eventually they established a rival religion.

The founder of Deism was Lord Herbert of Cherbury. Weary of the religious strife of his age, humanitarian, and skeptical, Herbert sought in natural religion a new basis for toleration. At the end of the seventeenth century, Deism was given a new vogue by a group of English pamphleteers. John Toland, the first "freethinker," published his *Christianity Not Mysterious* which asserted that the simple Christian religion (i.e., Deism) had been corrupted by priests who had invented mysteries to delude the people. Anthony Collins devoted himself to an attack on one of the standard arguments for Christianity, the evidence of prophecies and miracles. Matthew Tindal published a book whose title summarizes its theme: *Christianity as Old as Creation; or The Gospel a Republication of the Religion of Nature.* These works aroused a furious controversy; but Deistic ideas penetrated within the Church of England, where the dominant "latitudinarian" attitude tended to diminish the importance of doctrine and to emphasize simple morality and decency.

> For Modes of Faith let graceless zealots fight.
> His can't be wrong whose life is in the right.

Generally these tendencies were found compatible with a formal orthodoxy: as late as 1802, William Paley's *Natural Theology* became a standard textbook among Anglicans. However, as a by-product of Deism, anti-Trinitarian views grew in vogue; late in the century, most of the English Presbyterians and a few Anglicans formed a Unitarian Church which remains as the institutional embodiment of Deism.

By the 1740's, however, English Deism was losing its intellectual force. The concept of reason upon which the Deists relied was itself becoming subject to rational criticism. In the unique atmosphere of intellectual freedom characteristic of eighteenth-century Britain, even the defenders of the established church had to employ the weapons of reason to justify their position; and the Church of England was capable of producing spokesmen of the highest caliber. The debate centered around Locke's psychology of sensationalism. Bishop Berkeley advanced the startling idea that there was no necessary objective reality behind the sensations we perceive; the only reality is, not perceived matter, but the perceiving mind. This radical idealism was developed into an argument for the existence of God as the universal mind and a refutation of the implicit materialism in the Deist position. Another defender of Christianity was Bishop Butler, whose *Analogy of Religion* employed the double-edged argument that the credibility of natural religion was subject to the same objections that had been raised against Christian revelation; Christianity was no less reasonable and, on the whole, more probable. More striking, however, were the arguments of a non-Christian skeptic, David Hume. Hume had outdone the Deists in his refutation of miracles, suggesting ironically that "our most holy religion is founded on faith, not reason." But his *Essay Concerning Human Understanding* undercut a basic assumption of Lockeian psychology and hence of Deism, the notion of causality. Hume suggested that the "laws" of nature might be no more than habitual mental associations of things not actually connected. This skepticism was too corrosive even for the rationalists.

The leadership of the Deist cause passed from England to France, the cultural center of Europe. Here Deism took a more aggressive tone and merged with other streams of criticism directed against the Roman Catholic Church. The French *philosophes*—literally "philosophers" but more accurately publicists of the Enlightenment—attacked the bigotry and "superstition" which was symbolized by the institutional Church. Harassed by a sporadic censorship, they employed subtlety and indirection in their attacks, but they were no less effective on this account. Their famous *Encyclopedia* was permeated by hostility to the established religious order. The greatest of the *philosophes* was Voltaire, who masterfully employed humor as his weapon against the Church, with results more devastating than any frontal attack could attain. In his later years Voltaire devoted himself with passion—almost with fanaticism—to the struggle against intolerance; his motto was "crush the infamous thing," by which he meant both bigotry and the Church which supported it. Yet Voltaire's own Deistic religion was genuine: "Religion consists neither in the opinions of unintelligible metaphysics nor in vain display, but in adoration and in justice. To do good, that is his ceremony; to submit to God, that is his doctrine."

The ideas of the *philosophes* spread rapidly throughout educated Europe. One agency of dissemination was the secret brotherhood known as the Freemasons. This organization, which originated in England and included many eminent men, combined a Deistic belief in the "Great Architect of the Universe" with a secrecy and mystic ritual which perhaps compensated for the dryness of its rationalism. Freemasons were present wherever the ideas of the Enlightenment were advanced, and they were condemned by both the governments and the Church. Their importance has perhaps been exaggerated because of their secrecy: Freemasonry was an agency, not a source, of revolutionary ideas. Nonetheless, as positions hardened towards the end of the century, Continental Freemasonry became both positively anti-Christian and politically revolutionary, and from this source came many of the secret societies which were to menace churches and states in the nineteenth century.

In the latter part of the eighteenth century, the *philosophes* took two new courses. On the one hand, Deism tended to lose some of its harshly rationalistic character and to identify "natural religion" with the promptings of the heart rather than the head. Jean-Jacques Rousseau arrived at Deistic doctrines by consulting the emotions, and his sentimental Deism had a great vogue. Other writers, however, emphasized more strongly the mechanistic premises of rationalism, and they eventually abandoned Deism for a frank atheism. LaMettrie's *The Man-Machine* proposed a complete materialism; Helvetius' *On the Mind* advanced a purely utilitarian ethics; the Baron d'Holbach's *System of Nature* was perhaps the most powerful argument for atheism ever written. These men had only a small following, but they portended much for the future.

What defense could the Roman Catholic Church muster against these attacks by the leading intellectuals of the age? There were not lacking competent spokesmen of the Church: Pope Benedict XIV was a scholar and patron of learning, and St. Alphonsus Liguori was one of the greatest of moral theologians. The Jesuit editors of the *Journal de Trévoux* kept up a running fire against the *philosophes* on their own ground. However, the Roman Catholic replies to the Enlightenment were never as effective or as significant as the work of their Anglican counterparts. To complicate matters, the divisions within the Church were nearly as great a source of weakness as the vigor of its opponents.

One of the most profound sources of division within Roman Catholicism was a seventeenth-century heresy known as Jansenism. The posthumous *Augustinus* of Cornelius Jansen, Bishop of Ypres, revived extreme doctrines derived from St. Augustine on predestination and grace, approximating to the Calvinist position on these subjects. The moral fervor of Jansen's work won him many disciples, but in 1653 five Jansenist propositions were condemned by the Pope. The Jansenists displayed an amazing intellectual agility in evading Papal censures, arguing that the condemned propositions were not really Jansenist, questioning the Pope's authority in matters of fact, and finally taking refuge in an attitude of "respectful silence." Their resistance to Rome won them much sympathy from nationalistic Frenchmen, and their moral rigorism seemed to contrast favorably with the laxer doctrines of their Jesuit opponents. The controversy revived in 1713, when a Jansenist work was condemned by the Bull *Unigenitus*. The leading Jansenists were forced to submit, but Jansenist ideas survived among many of the clergy. The controversy had divided the French Church and created a habit of insubordination and independence of mind among both the lower clergy and the laity.

The most persistent opponents of Jansenism, and the most able and effective defenders of the Church on all issues, were the members of the Society of Jesus (Jesuits). Great missionaries, brilliant theologians, educators of the elite of the Catholic youth, and staunch critics of the Enlightenment, the Jesuits were especially effective among the upper classes. Their success brought them opposition both within and without the Church. Their direct obedience to the Pope offended both the diocesan clergy and the rulers of sovereign states, and their political activity brought upon them the charge that they sought to engross power. The *philosophes* regarded them as the chief enemy against whom a virtual crusade was preached: if the Jesuits could be crushed, the edifice they defended would surely fall. However, the effective blows against the Jesuits were delivered not by the *philosophes* but by the Catholic governments who regarded the tightly-organized Order as a source of resistance to the power of the state over its subjects. The Jesuits were expelled from Portugal in 1759, from France in 1764, from Spain, Naples and Parma in 1767. Diplomatic pressure was then applied to the Papacy to suppress the Order altogether; and finally, for the peace of the Church, the Society of Jesus was dissolved by Pope Clement XIV in 1773.

The suppression of the Jesuits was the greatest victory of the *philosophes* and the secular states over the Church in the eighteenth century. Perhaps the blow was misdirected: it has been the historic function of the Jesuits to take upon themselves the odium which properly belonged to the Church as a whole. Nonetheless, many historians regard their suppression as marking the nadir of the fortunes of Roman Catholicism in modern times.

The suppression of the Jesuits was a striking instance of the power of the secular states in religious affairs. This power had been decisive since the Reformation, when Protestant rulers assumed the government of the Church in their lands, and even those states which remained Catholic usually did so because it was the choice of their rulers. This ability to determine the faith of its subjects was an immense source of strength to the state. In Lutheran countries the abasement of the Church before the state was well-nigh complete. Some of the Calvinist churches, whose presbyterian polity encouraged a habit of self-government, were more successful in maintaining their autonomy, especially in Scotland; but even here the state had become, by the eighteenth century, the dominant partner. The Church of England had always been subordinated to the monarch, to whose effective powers Parliament succeeded. The brute fact of state control was elevated to a doctrine, Erastianism, which justified the concentration of the disciplinary power of the Church in the hands of the civil magistrate. Such a theory was similar to the "Caesaropapism" long practiced in the Byzantine and later the Russian empires. Significantly, the eighteenth century also marked a low point in the history of the Russian Orthodox Church. In 1721 Tsar Peter the Great suppressed the Patriarchate and proceeded to govern the Church as a department of the state through a Holy Synod presided over by a layman. This was the most extreme example of the tendency to deny independent authority to the Church.

Similar tendencies were at work in the Roman Catholic Church, even though that body had the advantage of a central authority at Rome independent of any state. In each Catholic country the monarch possessed, by concordat or custom, many powers over the Church, thus limiting the authority of the Pope, giving the local Church a distinctively national character, and making it in some measure an agency of the state. The extent of state control varied; it could never be complete as long as ties with Rome were maintained; but it was sufficient to provide frequent occasions of conflict between kings and Popes. Devout Catholicism did not appear to be incompatible with a practical independence of Roman authority. Thus the "most Catholic" kings of Spain obtained the right to nominate to bishoprics and major ecclesiastical benefices in Spain and complete powers of nomination in the colonies (*real patronato*); the Spanish Inquisition was an agency of the state, not the Church; and the monarchs exercised the power of approving decrees from Rome before these were allowed to be published in their domains (*placet*). Similar powers were held by the "most pious" kings of Portugal, with their extensive Asiatic and African empire. The Hapsburg rulers of Austria and Hungary held some of these powers, as did the Republic of Venice.

The tension between obedience to Rome and the autonomy of national Churches was most evident in France, where the "most Christian" kings had won, by the Concordat of Bologna (1516), the right of nominating bishops and abbots. Even before this, the French ("Gallican") Church had asserted its effective autonomy from Rome in matters of discipline and its subordination to the king in temporal affairs. This tradition of Gallicanism led to a direct conflict with Rome under Louis XIV—ironically, at the same time as he was expelling the Protestants from France. Louis was supported by the French bishops, led by the eloquent Bossuet, Bishop of Meaux, who had drawn a justification of absolute monarchy "from the very words of Scripture." In 1682 the bishops drew up a "Declaration of the clergy of France on the ecclesiastical power." They asserted that "kings and sovereigns are not subjected to any ecclesiastical power by the ordinance of God in temporal things" and cannot be deposed by the Pope; that the decrees of the Council of Constance (1414–1418), stating that Papal judgments may be reversed by general councils, remain in force; that the special rules and customs of local churches ought to retain their validity; and that, even in matters of faith, the Pope is not necessarily infallible. Had these doctrines been fully accepted, the Papacy would have been left with little more than a nominal primacy.

Gallicanism grew in strength in the eighteenth century, being reinforced by Jansenists hostile to Rome and by *philosophes* who looked to the all-powerful state to remedy the evils of society. From these influences came new movements opposed to the authority of the Pope. The most notable was Febronianism, so called from the pseudonym of its founder, Nikolaus von Hontheim, Coadjutor Bishop of Trier. "Febronius" asserted that the

Pope possessed no more than a primacy among his fellow-bishops; final authority rested in the Church as a whole acting through general councils. This conciliarist doctrine, similar to that of Constance, was modernized by an appeal to the monarchs to cooperate with the bishops in resisting Papal pretensions. Febronian doctrines were very influential, despite Papal condemnation, and were endorsed by the bishops of Tuscany at the Synod of Pistoia (1786). More important, they helped to provide a rationale for a new generation of monarchs bent on reasserting the powers of the state over the church in the interests of a general reform of society.

These monarchs were known as the "Enlightened Despots," because in some measure they accepted the progressive ideals of the Enlightenment; but quite often their policies were simply an extension of the old absolutism. They had in common a desire to effect social reforms by expanding the powers of the absolute bureaucratic state, of which the church was to be an agency. They were notable for their toleration: thus both Frederick the Great of Prussia and Catherine the Great of Russia, who had acquired territories inhabited by Roman Catholics, allowed the Jesuits to survive in their domains even after they had been suppressed by the Papacy. At the same time, these monarchs allowed the church no independent authority: Frederick insisted on the right to control all clerical appointments, and Catherine secularized the property of the Orthodox Church, rendering it dependent on state subsidies. The same tendencies were evident among monarchs of Catholic countries. Joseph I of Portugal, guided by his minister Pombal, had been the first to expel the Jesuits, and he introduced the secular ideas of the Enlightenment into education. Charles III of Spain curtailed clerical privileges and restricted the operations of the Inquisition.

The most thoroughgoing of the Enlightened Despots was the Holy Roman Emperor Joseph II, a *philosophe* enthroned. The ten years (1780–1790) of Joseph's sole rule in Austria and Hungary represented an attempt at social revolution imposed from above. In the religious sphere, Joseph decreed the legal equality of non-Catholics (including for the first time Jews) with Catholics, dissolved most of the monasteries, reduced the number of holy days, reorganized the dioceses, replaced diocesan seminaries with state institutions, and had the textbooks and catechisms rewritten. All this was accomplished by a series of decrees, without consultation with the hierarchy or with Rome. Pope Pius VI made the extraordinary gesture of coming in person to Vienna—an act symbolic of the diminished authority of the Papacy—but he failed to dissuade Joseph from his course. More effective was the resistance of Joseph's own subjects, who opposed his centralizing policies and eventually forced cancellation of most of his secular reforms; but many of his religious policies were retained by his successor Leopold II, who had earlier shown himself a reformer as Grand Duke of Tuscany.

Gallicanism, Febronianism, and Josephism were aspects of the general tendency to increase the power of the secular state at the expense of the independence of the Church. They coincided with an intellectual atmosphere which was secular and rationalistic, tending to weaken the role of religion in life and often to oppose the specific doctrines of Christianity. We should not exaggerate the impact of these forces: In the genteel eighteenth century issues were rarely pushed to extreme conclusions. The churches remained securely established, well endowed, externally prosperous and powerful; the clergy were respected and privileged members of society, to which they made an all-too-easy adjustment, rarely offering a determined resistance to the decrees of the monarchs. The new ideas were especially influential among the middle classes, the leading proponents of reforms; but the faith of the masses, so far as it can be determined, was not substantially affected by the doctrines of the *philosophes* or the encroachments of the states. Nonetheless, the net effect of all these tendencies, following upon a reaction from the religious tensions of the preceding era, was a decline in the vigor of the churches and a decay in the religious life of Europe.

This decline in religious fervor can be seen even in the attempts made to justify the Christian religion against its intellectual critics. It was significant that the ground of polemics had shifted from such subjects as grace and the sacraments to the basic issues of the validity of theism and the reasonableness of revelation. One wit remarked that nobody had questioned the existence of God until the apologists set out to prove it. The great Anglican apologists produced able justifications of a generalized Christianity; but it was one thing to prove that religion was credible and another to show that it was worth believing. Yet such writings as William Law's *Serious Call to a Devout and Holy Life* or Henry Dodwell's *Christianity not Founded on Argument,* which abandoned natural theology and relied on inner faith, were regarded as rather esoteric. The leading defenders of Christianity preferred to justify it as rational and natural, rather than as mysterious and supernatural.

Similarly, the sermons of the age had a rationalistic and uninspiring character. Of one eloquent French preacher it was remarked that, if he had only mentioned God, he would have treated every conceivable subject. For Anglicans the fashion was set by Archbishop Tillotson, whose favorite text was "His commandments are not grievous" and who approved the law of God because "it is suited to our nature and advantageous to our interest." Preachers tended to de-emphasize doctrine and to stress benevolence and morality, justified not as the command of God but on grounds of social utility and common sense. This rationalistic ethical theism, called "latitudinarianism" in England, permeated both Anglicanism and Nonconformity and found parallels on the Continent.

Under such circumstances, the devotional aspects of Christianity suffered. "Enthusiasm" came to be synonymous with fanaticism, and outward displays of religious feeling were considered socially *gauche.* Only in Germany did the devotional impulses of the seventeenth century continue in the form of Pietism. Even here there was a decline in later generations; thus the University of Halle, founded to promote Pietism, became a citadel of rationalism under the leadership of Christian Wolff.

The chief source of the diminished vigor of institutional Christianity in the eighteenth century was the complete involvement of the established churches in the existing social order. The age was one of apparent stability, comfort, and elegance for the upper classes. Society was dominated by a landed aristocracy which clung to its social privileges. The structure of the churches tended to conform to that of society. In Catholic countries, especially France, the higher offices of the Church were reserved for scions of the nobility, who were very well remunerated for services which often were nominal; meanwhile the parish clergy, usually drawn from the peasant class, were poorly paid. In the Church of England, although the structure was less rigid, social and political connection counted for more than devotion and talent. The right of patronage, by which landowners were often able to nominate parsons, tended to give the better-paid benefices to the younger sons of the gentry, while the humbler curates received minimal stipends. In Scotland the Kirk had traditionally been the most promising career for talented members of the lower classes; but patronage was reintroduced in the eighteenth century, with the consequence that both the militant Calvinism and the popular prestige of the clergy were reduced, and the stricter and more independent elements formed "secession" churches of their own. In nearly all countries a similar pattern prevailed: the more prosperous members of the clergy tended to accept the dominant secular values of society, while the poverty of the bulk of the clergy limited the extent of their influence. Such a system tended to discourage spirituality and to inhibit the churches from assuming an active and independent role.

Institutional Christianity could not recover its vigor until the churches were released from their entanglement with secular society, either by a revolution which would shake them from their social moorings or by a revival of piety among private individuals and groups. For such release the Roman Catholic Church had to wait until the French Revolution. For some branches of Protestantism, however, signs of a new life were already becoming evident in the course of the eighteenth century—in German Pietism, in the Methodist movement in England, in the Great Awakening in America—sources of that stream of evangelicalism which was to be one of the most vigorous expressions of Christianity in subsequent centuries. Even in the Age of the Enlightenment, new lines of activity and thought were being pursued which were ultimately destined to put an end to the calm and rational world of the eighteenth century.

3

Evangelical Revival

While the Enlightenment was running its course, a revolt was beginning against the rationalism and indifference which dominated the culture of the age. This revolt came from two sources. The first was the continuance into the eighteenth century, not in the highest circles of church and state but among private individuals, of strains of Puritanism, Pietism, and mysticism derived from the preceding epoch. The second was a reaction against two major premises of the Enlightenment: the sufficiency of human reason and the mechanistic order of nature. These two streams merged in the nineteenth century in a revival of the religious impulse which dramatically changed the situation of the churches.

In Protestantism the movement which largely shaped this revival is denoted by the term "evangelical." [1] In general, evangelical Protestantism represents a de-emphasis of the institutional and doctrinal aspects of Christianity in favor of the spiritual and

[1] The word "evangelical" (pertaining to the gospel) has been used with various meanings. At the time of the Reformation, it designated both Lutheran and Reformed elements; this usage has been superseded by "Protestant." In nineteenth-century Germany it was the name given to the state churches in which the Lutherans and Calvinists were merged. In England since the nineteenth century "evangelical" has been used to denote the "low-church" party in the Church of England. In America "Evangelical" is part of the names of several denominations which sprang from the evangelical revival.

moral transformation of the individual. It stresses a personal religious experience, often called "conversion," marked by consciousness of sin, awakening to grace, and commitment to the Christian life. Evangelical Protestants are characterized by moral earnestness, a rigorous standard of conduct, and frequent examination of conscience; they emphasize Bible reading, private family and group prayers, and an active role for the laity. They have become known for their organized efforts to influence and reform society, but the original emphasis of the movement was on individuals and small groups. At a time when the churches were failing to satisfy spiritual needs and when the traditional dogmatic approach was increasingly irrelevant to the intellectual tendencies of the age, the new emphases of evangelicalism were necessary to breathe fresh life into the Protestant churches.

Germany was the first to develop an evangelical movement, known as Pietism. In large measure Pietism was a revival of Luther's emphasis on salvation by faith and the priesthood of all believers. It represented a reaction against the tendency of Lutheran theologians to insist upon a narrow orthodoxy often called "Lutheran scholasticism." The father of German Pietism was Philip Jakob Spener, whose book *Pia Desideria* (1675) was a plea for church reform based on the experience of conversion, personal piety, Bible study and the activity of the laity. His most original contribution was the organization of small private groups (*collegia pietatis*) for devotional practices and the cultivation of the Christian life. To such methods the name Pietism was applied, at first in derision. Spener and a younger colleague, August Hermann Francke, were influential in the founding of the University of Halle, which became the intellectual center of Pietism in the early eighteenth century and trained thousands of pastors in the Pietistic spirit. Francke also developed the social activity of Pietism, founding an orphanage and several schools. After his death Halle became noted for rationalism rather than Pietism, but by then the movement had taken root elsewhere in Germany, most notably in Württemberg.

Pietism was reinforced by a group whose tradition antedated the Reformation itself, the Moravians. This body derived from

the Czech Hussites of the fifteenth century, whose radical wing
was accepted as Protestant at the time of the Reformation. They
were expelled from Bohemia and Moravia in the Thirty Years
War. Early in the eighteenth century, a small group of Moravian
refugees was given refuge at Herrnhut in Saxony by a local
nobleman, Count von Zinzendorf, who had been brought up in
Pietist circles. Under Zinzendorf's auspices the Moravians renewed their distinct ecclesiastical organization. In Europe they
sought to work within the Protestant state churches, bringing
fresh life and inspiration; on their own account they embarked
on missionary endeavors, especially in America, where a Moravian Church was successfully planted. Missionary activity was
generally a characteristic of Pietism. Halle was an important
missionary center, contributing to the shaping of the Lutheranism of the German immigrants to America.

Pietism spread beyond the limits of German Lutheranism. The
German and Swiss Reformed Churches bore traces of its influence. The Lutheran Church of Denmark and Norway was at
first receptive to Pietism, which influenced Bishop Pontopiddan,
who drew up the official catechism. Later, however, both in
Denmark-Norway and in Sweden, the development of Pietist
conventicles as potential rivals to the state churches alarmed the
governments, which issued several repressive edicts. There was,
indeed, a tendency among many Pietists toward a radical indi-
vidualism and free mysticism which often resulted in separation
from the state churches.

The decisive event in the history of evangelicalism was the
beginning of the Methodist movement in England. This rebirth
of the Puritan impulse began within the established Church of
England as a reaction against the cold, moralistic rationalism of
the day. The leaders were John and Charles Wesley and George
Whitefield. The Wesleys were the children of a High-Church
parson and his strong-willed wife, who drilled them in habits of
regularity and piety. As students at Oxford, they formed a "Holy
Club" whose methodical religious practices earned them the
name of Methodists, at first applied in derision. Whitefield

joined the group in 1735, in which year the Wesleys went out as missionaries to the new colony of Georgia. They were not successful, and John Wesley returned disheartened in 1738. On the voyage to Georgia, he had his first contact with the Moravians and was impressed by their quiet assurance, born of the experience of salvation by faith. Back in England, he renewed these contacts, seeking that personal experience which would give point to his combination of discipline and mysticism. This decisive experience of "conversion" came to Wesley at a prayer meeting on May 24, 1738, while listening to Luther's comments on justification by faith: "I felt my heart strangely warmed. I felt I did trust in Christ, Christ alone, for salvation; and an assurance was given me that he had taken away my sins, even mine, and saved me from the law of sin and death."

This warming of the heart, by which salvation by faith became a personal experience, was to be the model of evangelical conversions. It set Wesley on a course of active preaching, seeking to convey this experience to others. He preached the conscious acceptance of salvation and a consequent growth in holiness. The latter was developed into the most original element of Wesley's theology, the "second blessing" (after conversion) of holiness and perfect love of God. John Wesley was joined by his brother Charles, who became famous in his own right as a writer of hymns.

It was not Wesley's doctrine but his method of spreading it that gave to Methodism its distinctive characteristic. The impetus here came from Whitefield, who was working among the poor miners of Bristol and found it expedient to preach to crowds of them in the open fields rather than in churches. He appealed to Wesley to join him. Wesley was at first shocked by the novel method, thinking it almost a sin to save souls outside a church; but he found the technique effective. Open-field preaching became a necessity after Wesley found himself excluded from most Anglican pulpits owing to the clergy's distaste for his "enthusiasm." Boldly proclaiming the world his parish, he preached wherever he could find an audience, despite hostility which often led to violence. Open-field preaching made the success of the

Methodist movement. It made it possible for Wesley and Whitefield to reach the lower classes, who were left cold by moralistic
rationalism but could be stirred by an appeal to the emotions.
The religious hunger of the masses could find satisfaction in the
new preaching, which released powerful emotions. Sometimes,
indeed, the crudity of the popular response, as in the case of
physical convulsions, might be embarrassing; but in any case it
testified to the effectiveness of the preaching, at which Whitefield
especially excelled.

Whitefield began to diverge from Wesley as early as 1740. The
issue was theological. The experience of conversion, common to
all evangelicals, is capable of two different theological explana-
tions. Was conversion the free reception of grace by man, or was
it rather the working-out of a pre-ordained salvation? Wesley
adopted the first ("Arminian") explanation and found himself
opposed by Whitefield. The resulting rupture divided the evangelical forces, but it may also have contributed indirectly to extending their influence. Whitefield's "Calvinistic" views, which
seemed similar to traditional Puritanism, had more appeal than
Wesley's among that section of the Anglican clergy which was
later to be known as evangelical or "low church"; through them,
the evangelical movement was able to gain influence and dissemination in wider circles. Whitefield also worked effectively
among the Welsh, where his followers later organized themselves
as the Calvinistic Methodists. Thus the Methodist organization
developed by Wesley was far from the only expression of the
evangelical revival in Britain.

Wesley's genius lay in the field of organization. Outbursts of
religious enthusiasm had to be brought under discipline if the
result was to be a continuously effective Christian life. Wesley's
instinct for regularity combined with the lessons he had learned
from the Moravians, who had organized their converts into
"bands." Wesley placed converts on probation for a period of
time and organized them into "classes" under leaders who conducted weekly meetings. Eventually lay preachers emerged to
serve the local societies. As the movement grew, Wesley established "circuits" with traveling preachers and superintendents,

centralizing the whole in an annual conference of circuit preachers under his own autocratic direction. Wesley's organization was unique in its combination of local lay activity with centralized clerical control.

Wesley never intended to found a new church. He was an ordained minister of the Church of England, with a High Tory reverence for authority and liturgy, who had been driven to develop a new religious organization almost by default. The Methodist "connection," as he termed it, was intended merely as a supplement to the work of the established Church, filling a religious gap that had been created by official neglect. Yet the "connection" imperceptibly developed all the characteristics of a distinct denomination. By Wesley's death in 1791 it numbered over 70,000 members, with a nearly equal number in America, to which missionaries had been sent. The circuit preachers and local leaders and stewards provided nearly all the services of religion except for the formal administration of sacraments, and only Wesley's insistence restrained them from that. By commissioning preachers on his own authority, Wesley had placed himself in an awkward position: his "connection" was virtually an *imperium in imperio* within the Church of England. He was slow to recognize this until the separation of the American colonies from England forced his hand. The American Methodists had no further use for the Church of England and demanded clergy of their own. In 1784, Wesley ordained two presbyters for the American church. Wesley later ordained other clergy for Scotland and England. Such acts on the part of a simple priest were in violation of the canons of the Anglican Church and foreshadowed an ultimate separation. Also in 1784 Wesley provided for the future government of the Methodist "connection" by deeding his authority to a Conference of one hundred preachers. Nonetheless, Wesley remained within the Church of England until his death. Shortly thereafter, the Wesleyan Methodist Church was effectively constituted as a separate denomination.

No sooner had the Methodist Church achieved its independence than it too became subject to secessions. The Conference which succeeded to Wesley's authority was exclusively composed of preachers and maintained a rigidly centralized control of the organization. Seeking respectability, the Conference adopted a conservative position in politics and discouraged spontaneous movements among the membership. Yet the tendency of the local societies was democratic; indeed, for many of the lower classes the Methodist societies were their first experience in self-government. Out of this conflict, three new, smaller denominations appeared. In 1797 the Methodist New Connection was formed by those who wished to admit laymen to a share in the government of the sect. In 1818 another denomination, the Bible Christians, was formed on the same basis. Meanwhile in 1812 there appeared the Primitive Methodists, composed of those who sought to renew the original enthusiasm of Methodism through such revivalistic methods as camp meetings.

Repeated secessions, however, did not prevent Wesleyan Methodism from growing rapidly, especially among the more active elements of the working class in an increasingly industrialized society. An eminent historian, Elie Halévy, has suggested that the rise of Methodism was largely responsible for the fact that the English working class was not led into a revolution such as occurred in France. While this view is exaggerated, it is certain that Methodism was a stabilizing influence on a distressed class in a period of increasing social tension.

The Methodists added new strength to the ranks of the nonconformist churches of England. The older dissenting bodies, losing the original Puritan fervor, had been declining throughout the eighteenth century. The Methodists became the largest of the nonconformist denominations. Perhaps stimulated by the competition, some of the older bodies, notably the Baptists and Congregationalists, bestirred themselves, adopted some of the evangelistic techniques of the Methodists, and experienced a revival of their strength. They were especially effective among the middle classes, growing in numbers and power in this period and eventually destined to set the tone of English life in the nineteenth century. The older dissenting bodies provided channels through which the evangelical spirit could inform the "respectable" classes who were not as easily reached by the Methodists.

It was, however, through elements within the established Church itself that evangelicalism was to become the decisive religious force in nineteenth-century England. The Puritan element in the Church of England, although submerged in the eighteenth century, had never been completely eliminated. There were some clergymen who supported the work of Wesley and Whitefield. One such was John Newton, curate of Olney, whose most famous parishioner was the poet William Cowper; both men were notable writers of hymns. The influence of Whitefield was greater than that of Wesley on such men, who were inclined to a moderate Calvinism. By the end of the century, a definite evangelical movement was effectively at work within the Anglican Church.

One center of this movement was at Cambridge, where the university produced two great evangelical leaders, Isaac Milner, professor of science and head of a college, and Charles Simeon, vicar of Holy Trinity Church. Simeon set himself to the work of training young men for their duties as ministers, so that Cambridge became a virtual seminary for evangelical clergymen. The second center of the evangelical movement was the London suburb of Clapham, whose parish church was served by members of the eminent Venn family. Around this church gathered a remarkable group of influential laymen of the upper middle class who became known as the "Clapham sect." Their leader was William Wilberforce, Tory member of Parliament, who led the campaign which resulted in the abolition of the slave trade (1807) and of slavery itself (1833). This was the most striking and successful of the many philanthropic projects to which the Clapham group dedicated themselves. They were active in the formation of Bible societies, missionary societies, and Sunday schools. Another celebrity of the evangelical movement was Hannah More, a prolific writer of religious works. The publication of such "tracts" was a notable feature of British evangelicalism.

The evangelicals remained a relatively small minority within the Church of England until well into the nineteenth century. They met considerable resistance from the latitudinarian higher clergy—sometimes called the "high and dry" party. The first evangelical to become a bishop was appointed in 1815, and for a long time he stood alone. The evangelicals were more numerous among the parish clergy, due partly to Simeon's recruiting and partly to the effective use of their patronage by wealthy Clapham- ites. The evangelicals became a distinct party within the Church of England, propagandizing so effectively that their influ- ence came to be far greater than their numbers would indicate. In many of their endeavors they worked closely with like-minded nonconformists, for the evangelical movement transcended de- nominational boundaries; but they enjoyed their peculiar influ- cnce precisely because they remained and worked within the established Church.

In the nineteenth century, evangelicalism was to become the most vital religious force in England. This was partly due to the class basis on which it rested. Although Wesley and Whitefield worked effectively among the poor, and Clapham included gentry and aristocrats, evangelicalism drew its strength from the middle classes, who reached the height of their power in this new industrial era. The evangelical combination of sober morality and active service was the fittest expression of the practical reli- gion of the successful middle class. Bourgeois respectability, sanc- tified by evangelical religion, subdued both the once-dissolute aristocracy and the rising elements of the proletariat. It showed itself at its best in the renewed emphasis on the sanctity of the family. Family prayers and strict observance of the Sabbath were perhaps the most distinctive institutions of British evangelical- ism. The contrast with the laxer ways of the eighteenth century was refreshing.

The most notable achievements of the English evangelicals were in the field of philanthropic endeavor. They sought not merely individual holiness but the sanctification of the nation. For this purpose they worked energetically through the voluntary societies characteristic of the time, and also through the gov- ernmental action which made the nineteenth century the "age of reform." They promoted the mission societies which commenced the modern missionary outreach of Protestantism. They were largely responsible for the abolition of slavery. Their main work, however, was at home with the working classes, whose numbers were increased and whose distress was made evident by the Industrial Revolution. The primary interest of the evangelicals was in the moral welfare of the "lower orders." Regarding education as a necessary preliminary to morality, they promoted schools for the poor; they distributed free Bibles and religious tracts. Later they were to work for reform of the hours and conditions of labor in mines and factories. The finest product of the evangelical impulse was a diffused humanitarianism which eventually affected many who did not subscribe to evangelical religion as such.

Yet there is something patronizing in even the most genuine humanitarianism. The Anglican evangelicals worked for the poor, but not with them. The "lower orders" were exhorted to be content in "that station of life in which they have been placed by God" and to seek relief for their sufferings in a future life rather than in any improvement of their earthly condition. Wilberforce wrote of the "more lowly path" of the poor:

> It is their part faithfully to discharge its duties and contentedly to bear its burdens . . . The peace of mind which Religion affords indiscriminately to all ranks affords more true satisfaction than all the expensive pleasures that are beyond the poor man's reach.

This was the natural attitude of the middle and upper classes to which the evangelical reformers belonged; but it is possible that some of the Clapham group saw their work as a deliberate attempt to head off a revolt of the lower classes. Significantly, evangelicalism did not receive as warm a response from the very lowest elements in the social scale as it did from the middle classes.

It is difficult to assess the causal factors in the development of the evangelical movement in England. All that is certain is that the growth of evangelicalism and the rise of industrialism coincided in time, and during that time England escaped the sort of revolution which occurred in France. Most likely, factors other than religious were decisive in shaping the social and political history of England in the period of rapid industrialization (c.

1760–1830). Yet the character of the nation in the Victorian period which followed bore the powerful impress of the evangelical spirit.

Even more than England, the British North American colonies were affected by the evangelical revival. Some of the colonies, particularly in New England, had their roots in seventeenth-century Puritanism; but the original fervor was lost by succeeding generations. In several other colonies the Church of England was established, but only a minority of the population were members. Few religious services were available on the expanding frontier. The need and opportunity for revival were evident in America; and evangelical Protestantism, by carrying through such a revival, became the dominant religious force in the United States.

The first stage of the revival was the phenomenon known as the Great Awakening. The preaching of Jonathan Edwards, the greatest Calvinist theologian produced by America, brought about a wave of conversions in 1734–1735, and the movement thus begun was reinforced by several preaching tours of the colonies by Whitefield. The momentum of the revival slackened after mid-century, but it had given impetus to the rapid growth of the Baptist and Methodist denominations. After the Revolutionary War, a second series of revivals commenced, characterized by the new technique of the camp meeting. Mass evangelism became a regular part of the American religious scene, and the work of reclaiming the unchurched majority was carried forward. Church establishments were abolished, to be replaced in time by an evangelical consensus.

In the countries which it had affected, evangelicalism brought back the spark of life to dormant Protestant churches. Beginning as an attempt to enliven stagnant establishments, it developed into a popular movement, particularly in England and America. The significance of evangelicalism lay in its direct appeal to the individual. Despite its social activism, evangelicalism was a personal religion, de-emphasizing church and community and stressing the individual's consciousness of the state of his soul. This personal rather than social morality was deficient in several ways which the nineteenth century would reveal. However, in the late eighteenth century, as a protest against the stagnation of established churches, and in the early nineteenth century, as a means of adjustment in a rapidly changing society, the individualism of the evangelical revival was a source of strength. The appeal from the church to the individual, from society to the soul, was a renewal of the spirit of the Reformation.

4

The Revolutionary Era

The French Revolution begins a new epoch in Church history
in which the issues are vaster and more urgent. Despite its intellectual debates and political quarrels, the eighteenth century had
been a period of social and institutional stability in which the
established churches rested secure in their privileged positions.
Now came a cataclysm which assailed the foundations of the
entire social order to which the churches had become so comfort-
ably attached. In the effort to reconstruct the world on the principles of reason and liberty, the Revolution swept away much of
the old order, leaving the churches adrift on a stormy sea, far
from their accustomed moorings. Since Catholic countries were in
the direct path of the storm, the Revolution struck most immediately at the Roman Catholic Church; the effect on Protestantism
was largely indirect, by way of reaction. But the new movements
to which the various stages of the Revolution gave birth—liberalism, democracy and nationalism—posed challenges to all the
churches in the course of the nineteenth century. The Revolution swept through Europe like a cleansing fire, clearing away
much that was already moribund, but effecting no final solution
and leaving an empty space into which rushed a multitude of
competing forces, both new and old. In this turmoil into which
they had so suddenly been thrust, the churches had to make their
way.

France, the "eldest daughter of the Church," was to strike the first blow at the old edifice. The Catholic clergy of France composed the "First Estate" of the realm, endowed with social privileges, exclusive official recognition, immunity from direct taxation, and a great wealth derived from tithes and the ownership of about one-tenth of the land. The Church was thoroughly—indeed too much—an accepted part of the social order. Linked with the nobility, whose scions held the higher ecclesiastical offices, the clergy formed part of the privileged minority of the nation whose refusal to adjust its status brought on the Revolution.

By the eighteenth century, the discrepancy between the spiritual aspirations of the Catholic faith and the worldly ease of the French hierarchy was patent. To be sure, the accounts of moral corruption can be exaggerated: if there were unbelieving bishops and amorous *abbés,* other dignitaries were at least conscientious, and the lives of the parochial clergy were exemplary. Indeed, the virtues of the lower clergy made most evident the need for a reform of the superstructure of the Church. While the nobility monopolized the higher dignities of the Church and enjoyed most of its wealth, the parish priests (*curés*), who carried on the daily work of religion and held the respect of their parishioners, were scandalously underpaid. Drawn from the lower classes and living often at a level not better than that of the peasants, the lower clergy naturally tended to identify their interests with the common laity of the Third Estate and not with their ecclesiastical superiors. Some of the lower clergy were attracted to Jansenism or to the doctrines of Edmond Richer, an early Gallican theologian who had emphasized the divine commission of priests as well as of bishops. Such doctrines tended to create a division within the clerical body; and many priests regarded the revolutionary events of 1789 as an opportunity to effect a needed reform of the Church.

The majority of the deputies of the First Estate were chosen from the lower clergy, and they joined with the Third Estate in the constitutional conflict which marked the opening of the Revolution. After the victory of the Third Estate which their support had helped to achieve, most of the clerical deputies continued to support revolutionary legislation. At the famous session of the night of August 4, 1789, in which the structure of feudalism and class privilege was abolished, the clergy agreed to renounce their tithes and fees. The Revolution, whatever its Enlightenment antecedents, was not initially directed against the Church, and the members of the National Assembly professed adherence to Catholicism; but state and Church were too intimately associated for one to be reorganized while the other remained unaffected. In September, the Declaration of the Rights of Man guaranteed religious toleration, despite some clerical protests, and the surviving Huguenots emerged from a century of legal oblivion. In November, all the property of the Church was declared "at the disposal of the nation," and church lands were to be sold to provide backing for the new paper currency (*assignats*). In return, the nation assumed the obligation of providing adequate financial support for the clergy. This obligation, however, gave the state an opportunity to interfere directly in ecclesiastical matters. The necessary reconstruction of Church finances provided the occasion for a reorganization of the Church itself. In February, 1790, monastic vows and religious orders were suppressed, although establishments for education and charity were kept open. Then the Assembly turned its attention to the general organization of the Church in France.

The Civil Constitution of the Clergy (July 12, 1790) drastically reorganized the French Church as part of a general reconstruction of society on the basis of secularist rationalism. The number of dioceses was reduced from 135 to 85, corresponding to the newly-established civil departments, and superfluous ecclesiastical dignities were suppressed. Bishops and *curés* were to be chosen by the electors, including non-Catholics, of their districts. Bishops were to be instituted in office without the need of confirmation by the Pope, but they were to inform him of their election "in testimony of the unity of faith and communion." The salaries of priests were fixed at an improved level. The Civil Constitution afforded the parochial clergy a considerable victory over the bishops and the religious orders, and in its disregard of Roman authority it was an expression of the Gallicanism common to all elements in the French Church. But these intra-ecclesiastical victories were purchased at the price of the independence and integrity of the Church, for the Civil Constitution was imposed unilaterally by decree of the State, acting on the doctrine of unlimited popular sovereignty, without consultation with Church authorities either in France or in Rome.

Would the Civil Constitution be accepted by the clergy? The issue divided the French Church. The National Assembly, anxious to test the loyalty of the clergy, required them to take an oath to uphold the Constitution. Nearly all the bishops, followed by many priests, refused, thereby forfeiting their offices. About half the secular clergy, of whom some later recanted, took the oath. Elections were held for the vacant sees, the new bishops being consecrated by the few who had accepted the new order, notably the unscrupulous Talleyrand of Autun.[1] A schism had developed between the "constitutional" and the "non-juring" clergy when the Pope finally pronounced against the Civil Constitution. In the Bull Caritas (1791), Pius VI condemned the clerical oath and invalidated the new consecrations, suspending priests and bishops who had collaborated in either.

The Pope's decision was an almost inevitable response to the French state's attack on the independence of the Church; but his intransigence resulted in an irreparable breach between the Church and the victorious Revolution and set the seal on the French schism. Devout Catholics, including King Louis XVI, were forced to choose between their consciences and the Revolution. Most of them adhered to the "good priests" who had refused the oath, and the clergy of the Constitutional Church found themselves unsupported by their parishioners and increasingly dependent on the state. Roman Catholicism became a focus of opposition to the Revolution, and the revolutionaries in turn were driven to take more drastic steps against the Church. Such were the consequences of the Civil Constitution of the Clergy, probably the greatest blunder of the French Revolution.

The result of this external pressure and internal schism was

[1] Talleyrand later abandoned the Church and went on to fame as a diplomat. He was famous for his ability to join the winning side at the decisive moment. On his deathbed, he was reconciled to the Church.

the effective disruption of the religious life of France. Many clergymen, especially in the higher ranks, fled from France, joining the aristocratic *émigrés* who were urging the governments of Europe to join in a crusade to restore the old order. The nonjuring clergy who remained in France were subject to increasing persecution and, when war broke out in 1792, were ordered to be deported. The Constitutional Church, despite its official status, never succeeded in establishing its position and eventually was abandoned by the revolutionaries who had instituted it. As the Revolution proceeded through its more radical stages—the monarchy was overthrown in 1792 and the Reign of Terror commenced in 1793—every institution of religion in France fell before the storm. The Roman Catholic Church had identified itself with the counter-revolution—the formidable royalist rising of the peasants of the Vendée was largely religious in its inspiration—and the revolutionaries, fearful of invasion from without and treason within, struck blindly at the clergy. Priests awaiting deportation were among the victims of the massacres of September, 1792; the remaining non-jurors were declared "suspects" along with the aristocrats; and, before the Terror came to an end, hundreds of priests and religious had died beneath the guillotine or in prison.

As more radical elements came to the fore, the latent anti-Christianity of the Revolution found increasing scope. A Revolutionary calendar was adopted, dispensing with Sundays and holy days. Extremists in Paris forced the Constitutional bishop, Gobel, to resign and, in November, 1793, instituted the worship of the Goddess of Reason in the person of a young woman of doubtful virtue enthroned in the cathedral of Notre Dame. Reacting against this atheism, the great terrorist Robespierre, inspired by the Deism of Rousseau, inaugurated in 1794 a civil religion of the "Supreme Being." Under these pressures the Constitutional Church collapsed, many of its bishops apostatizing and some marrying; by the spring of 1794 Mass was said in less than 200 parishes.

In the reaction which followed the fall of Robespierre (July, 1794), the persecution of the Church abated. In 1795, the Constitutional Church, now disestablished, was left free to conduct worship; Catholics who submitted to the Republic were allowed to re-occupy some churches; and the Vendée was pacified by a grant of religious liberty. The surviving non-jurors emerged from their hiding-places, reinforced by some returned *émigrés*, and Catholic worship was restored in most parishes, though the schism remained unhealed. The Directory which now governed France was still anti-clerical, maintaining a Deistic state cult, and the persecution was renewed in 1797, but it was neither as severe nor as effective as before. The remarkable resilience of the Church, despite its grievous losses, showed that the Roman Catholic faith had not entirely lost its hold on the bulk of the population. It now remained to reach a *modus vivendi* between the new political order and the old religion.

The effects of the Revolution had not been confined to France. In 1791, the Papal territory of Avignon, an enclave in southern France, was annexed by order of the National Assembly—an early instance of the conflict of nationalism with the Church. In the course of the Revolutionary wars (1792–1797), Belgium and the German Rhineland fell to the French armies; the anti-religious policy was extended to these Catholic districts, and the estates of the clergy were confiscated and sold. As the war extended into Italy it reached the borders of the Papal States, and the Pope, who had joined in the war against France, was forced to sign the humiliating Treaty of Tolentino (1796), paying an indemnity and ceding some of his territories. The unhappy Pius VI, one of the most conciliatory of Popes, had to suffer further indignities. In 1798, an incident gave the French army an excuse to occupy Rome; the Pope was deposed as a temporal ruler and exiled, first to Siena and then by stages to Valence in France. There, in August, 1799, the worn-out old man died, a prisoner of the French Republic. His successor, Pius VII, was elected after much delay in Venice, under the protection of Austria.

The suffering of the Church was ended by the coming to power of Napoleon Bonaparte as First Consul of France in 1799. Napoleon himself was virtually devoid of religious sentiment, but he recognized the influence of religion over the people and its utility as an instrument of social control. His immediate mission was to restore peace and stability in France, and for this it was necessary to come to a *rapprochement* with the Church. Beginning cautiously with a lightening of restrictions and with partial amnesties, his approaches were met in a conciliatory spirit by the brilliant new Papal Secretary of State, Ercole Consalvi. After much negotiation, an agreement was reached, the Concordat of 1801.

The Concordat terminated the strife between the Church and the Republic. The Roman Catholic faith was recognized as "the religion of the great majority of French citizens," though not as the religion of the state. Both the Church of the Old Regime and the new Constitutional Church were superseded by the new arrangements: the schism was to be healed by the forced resignations of the bishops of both groups.[2] In the future, all bishops were to be nominated by the head of the French government, and the Pope was to confirm their canonical authority. The bishops were to appoint the parish clergy. Ecclesiastics were to take an oath of allegiance to the government and to offer prayers for it. The Pope recognized the confiscation and sale of the former church lands. In turn, the government placed at the disposal of the bishops all unsold church buildings needed for worship, and the state was to pay the salaries of the clergy. The free exercise of the Roman Catholic religion was assured, subject to "the police regulations which the government shall deem necessary for the public tranquillity."

The Concordat was a compromise largely favorable to Rome. Catholic worship had been restored in France with public support, and the schism was ended. The wholesale deposition of bishops was a direct exercise of Papal authority in France which shattered at one blow the Gallican theory of the autonomy of the French Church. The immediate authority of the Pope over the bishops, and of the bishops over the clergy, made the Church a more disciplined body. At the same time, the power of the state

[2] Some of the pre-Revolutionary bishops, asserting the traditional immunities of the Gallican Church, refused to resign, forming a small new schism, the *petite église,* which lasted to 1893.

over the Church was increased. The clergy depended for their support on state salaries rather than their own property; the bishops were the appointees of the head of the state and were thus unlikely to display independence. The provision for "police regulations" allowed Napoleon to enact the "Organic Articles," which in many respects nullified the Papal gains. These Articles forbade acts of the Holy See or of general councils to be published in France without the permission of the government, required governmental consent to the exercise of authority by Papal officials or the holding of provincial councils or synods, regulated chapters, seminaries and some aspects of worship, and obliged seminary professors to subscribe to the Gallican declaration of 1682. The "Organic Articles" were published as an integral part of the Concordat, although the Pope had not agreed to them and indeed issued a protest.

It was evident that Napoleon considered the Church primarily as an agency of state control, serving to render the population submissive and obedient. In the "Imperial Catechism" which was issued in 1807, children were taught that, under pain of damnation, "Christians owe to the princes who govern them, and we owe in particular to Napoleon I, our Emperor, love, respect, obedience, fidelity, military service and the tributes laid for the preservation and defence of the Empire." This was far from the intention of Pius VII in agreeing to the Concordat; but the Pope continued to be conciliatory in the interests of peace. In 1804 he was even persuaded to come to Paris for the coronation of Napoleon as Emperor, giving his sanction to the new regime.

The concordatory arrangements were extended to other countries to which French influence had penetrated. The Concordat itself was necessarily applied to those areas annexed by France, which included Belgium, the Rhineland and Piedmont in Italy; a similar arrangement was concluded for a French puppet state in northern Italy. The most striking effects of the post-Revolutionary readjustment were found in Germany. Here the Roman Catholic bishops were also territorial princes whose wealth was at once a temptation to the secular rulers and a hindrance to their own spiritual mission. Some of the ecclesiastical territories in the

Rhineland had been lost to France in the Revolutionary wars, in which also several secular princes were dispossessed. The latter arranged for themselves to be compensated by taking over the remaining ecclesiastical states. The re-arrangement, consummated in 1803, put an end to the ecclesiastical principalities and forced a reorganization of the Church in Germany which was not completed until after the Napoleonic era had ended. A large proportion of the Roman Catholics of Germany found themselves subject to Protestant rulers. Each state, including Catholic Bavaria, undertook the reorganization of the Church in its territories, reducing it to the status of an agency of the government. Religion and education were to be supported by state salaries; church lands were secularized and monasteries dissolved; the supervision of religious affairs was entrusted to civil bureaucrats. So confused was the condition of the Church in Germany (over half the sees were vacant) that no resistance could be made. Indeed, the one ecclesiastical ruler who was permitted for a time to retain his principality, the Prince-Primate Dalberg, influenced by his Vicar-General, Wessenberg, sponsored projects of an autonomous German Catholic Church which created some alarm at Rome.

Rome had more to fear, however, from Napoleon, whose insatiable ambition eventually nullified the conciliatory efforts of Pius VII. In the course of his war with Britain, Napoleon sought to unite the states of Europe into his "Continental System," which would shut off the markets for British goods. The Pope, as ruler of a territorial state, was required to join in the System; but Pius, anxious to preserve his neutrality, refused to do so. In 1808, Napoleon's troops occupied Rome; and in May, 1809, the Papal States were annexed to the French Empire, the Pope being deposed as a temporal ruler. Pius replied by excommunicating Napoleon as a despoiler of the Church, whereupon Napoleon had the Pope arrested and imprisoned, first at Savona and later at Fontainebleau; many of the cardinals and Italian bishops were also imprisoned. The Pope could only reply by refusing to perform any pontifical functions, thereby preventing Napoleon from filling vacant episcopal sees. The imprisonment of Pius

VII, only a decade after the death in prison of his predecessor, seemed to have reduced the Church to a state as low as it had been in before the Concordat.

Relief came in sight when Napoleon, overreaching himself, began to suffer defeats in his wars after 1812. In Spain, the Church became the focus of the national resistance to Napoleon. He began negotiating with the Pope, offering to restore the Papal States; but the conditions were unacceptable. Negotiation was rendered unnecessary by the fall of Napoleon in 1814. The Pope returned to Rome; and Consalvi secured the restoration nearly intact of the Papal States. "Restoration," indeed, was the watchword of the post-Napoleonic period, and the Roman Catholic Church gained much from this situation, being regarded as one of the pillars of order and stability. If it had suffered severely, it had at least survived; and amidst the fall of so many old institutions, survival itself was an accomplishment.

The Protestant churches were less severely affected by the Revolutionary and Napoleonic struggles. The Protestants of France indeed benefitted, being granted not merely toleration but equality. Napoleon required the Calvinists and Lutherans each to form a central organization for France and placed them under a governmental control similar to that provided for the Roman Catholic Church.[3] In general, however—except in the Netherlands and parts of Germany, where some dislocation was experienced—the Protestant countries were out of the path of the storm. In England, as part of the patriotic reaction against France, there was a notable revival of Protestant worship, which merged with the evangelical movement; here the effect of the Revolution was indirectly to strengthen religion, which was regarded as a bulwark of the social order. Movements which arose earlier than and independently of the Revolution, such as evangelicalism in England and Romanticism in Germany, were more influential in shaping Protestantism in this era.

The French Revolution, however, was but the first of many revolutions which were to take place in the next century, and no

[3] A similar arrangement was made for the Jews.

church was to remain immune from the cumulative effects of the revolutionary age. A precedent had been set for the shattering of old institutions; the peace of Europe had been violently disturbed. For millions of people, the habits of traditional religious observance had been broken, and it was not easy to revive them.

5

The Reaction Against the Enlightenment

The era which succeeded the Revolutionary and Napoleonic wars is known as the "Restoration." Never was a name more inappropriate. Eighteenth-century society had been shattered and could not be restored; and the intellectual world of the Enlightenment had been discredited by the Revolution for which it had prepared the way. The Enlightenment and the Revolution were dissolvent forces which had done their work too well. Europe, weary of strife, now sought principles of order, stability, and authority. In politics, the new tendency is known as the conservative reaction; in intellectual affairs, it is called Romanticism. In either case it represented a reaction against the tendencies of the preceding age. This was a mood most propitious for the cause of religion. The religious revival of the first half of the nineteenth century was an integral part of the reaction against the eighteenth century.

On the political side, this reaction took the form of the restoration of absolutist monarchies and the formation of a conservative ideology. The doctrine of conservatism was the product of the reaction against the French Revolution. This can be clearly seen in the case of Britain, the most liberal state of the eighteenth century, which became the most consistent opponent of revolutionary France. Patriotism and religion were both enlisted in the defense of the established order against the revolutionary menace. The spokesman of English Conservatism was Edmund

Burke, a politician who had earlier been regarded as a moderate reformer. Shocked by the excesses of the French revolutionaries, Burke published his *Reflections on the Revolution in France* (1790), denouncing both the Revolution and the doctrines of the Enlightenment which he regarded as its cause. Instead of the abstract rationalist principles of the Enlightenment, Burke argued that men should be guided by their sentiments and instincts, which instilled devotion to traditions and established institutions. He struck a responsive chord by his recognition of the aridity of the Enlightenment's reliance on the "mere reason" of the individual; he appealed from the head to the heart, to those sentiments and instincts which bound men together in society. Burke was a frank irrationalist who conceived of society as a mystic union evolving over a long period of time, transcending the wills of individuals, and worthy of reverence as an embodiment of a higher purpose than the immediate interests of those who composed it. Religion was called upon to give a divine sanction to the state and to instill in men the sense of reverence necessary to stabilize the social order. Hence Burke exalted religion: "We know, and what is better, we feel inwardly that religion is the basis of civil society. . . .We know, and it is our pride to know, that man is by his constitution a religious animal; that atheism is against, not only our reason, but our instincts; and that it cannot prevail long."

On the Continent, the union of conservatism with religion was propounded in less poetic but equally powerful form by a Savoyard diplomat, Count Joseph de Maistre. Where Burke had based conservatism on tradition, de Maistre based it on the need for authority. The lesson de Maistre learned from the Revolution was that the evil inherent in man's nature could not be restrained except by an absolute authority in both the moral and the temporal spheres. The State and the Church, the hangman and the priest, were divinely commissioned to maintain order. De Maistre justified monarchical absolutism as the only alternative to chaos. In the Roman Catholic tradition, his picture of the universe was hierarchical, and so the absolute State was to be subordinated to the universal Church, headed by an absolute and infallible Pope: "No national character without religion. . . . No Christianity without Catholicism, and no Catholicism without the Pope." In his great work *Du Pape* (1819), de Maistre set forth his ideal of a Christian world under Papal authority.

This Ultramontanism—looking "over the mountains" to the authority of the Pope in Rome—became the keynote of the Roman Catholic revival. In proportion as individual reason came to be regarded as the source of the errors of the Enlightenment and the Revolution, Catholic thinkers exalted the infallible authority of the Church and its head. The Vicomte de Bonald propounded the doctrine of "traditionalism," denigrating individual reason and relying on the traditions of the Church. The *Essay on Indifference* (1817) of Félicité de Lamennais asserted that the principle of private judgement was the source of the errors of the Revolution; individual reason was impotent, and the test of truth was the universal reason of mankind, which is embodied in the tradition of the Church as expressed by the Pope. The excesses of these doctrines were later condemned by the Church, whose scholastic philosophy is itself rationalistic and holds that reason has a legitimate function in religion; but they left as a permanent residue a heightened sense of the authority of the Church and the role of authority within the Church. In their anti-intellectualism they were in tune with their times and merged in the larger movement of reaction against the Enlightenment which is known as Romanticism.[1]

It is as impossible to define Romanticism as it is to ignore it. The term is used, often very loosely, to denote a variety of impulses and movements which together shaped the modes of thought characteristic of the early nineteenth century. Generally these movements represented reactions against the classicist art forms or the rationalistic doctrines of the preceding century, which were now regarded as narrow and restrictive. Such reactions might take a variety of expressions, often mutually contra-

[1] Another anti-intellectualist philosophy was the "fideism" of Abbé Louis Bautain, who held that reason was incompetent in metaphysics and that knowledge of God could come only through faith and immediate insight. Bautain was required to sign a formula of recantation in 1840.

dictory. What they had in common was a striving after the fullest possible range of human experience and imagination, particularly those elements which transcend rational formulation. Two characteristics of Romanticism stand out relatively clearly: the emphasis on the less rational aspects of human life, and a new anti-abstract vision of nature. Men now wanted something more than "mere" reason could supply; they appealed from the rational understanding to instinct and sentiment. This inner consciousness was not a mechanical response to objective sensations but rather a living thing, which could penetrate into a new world of experience unknown to the self-limited rationalism of the Enlightenment. The result was a new vision of nature, not as an abstract, uniform, mechanistic system, but as an organic process, characterized by variety, irregularity, change, and complexity. Romanticists rejoiced in the unclassifiable, in extremes and opposites, in things which were too exotic, or too humble, to have been comprehended by the cool rational world of the eighteenth century. The Romantic movement was thus as diffuse in its interests and expressions as is the free-ranging mind of man. Starting as a literary protest, of which Goethe, Schiller, Wordsworth, and Coleridge were the early protagonists, it came to have ramifications in art, music, history, politics, philosophy, and religion.

The change in intellectual fashions, substituting sentiment for reason as the ultimate test of truth, gave a chance for intellectual respectability to Christian faith, which is ultimately superrational in its appeal. In a significant reversal of value-judgments, the eighteenth-century grounds of criticism of Christianity—its reliance on the non-rational, on authority, on tradition, on ritual and on institutional establishment—were now cited as arguments in its favor. Thus the prophet of Romanticism in France, the Vicomte de Chateaubriand, was also the herald of the Catholic revival; in his *Genius of Christianity* (1802), he defended the Christian faith primarily on the ground of its "beauty." It was no longer necessary to rely on rationalistic "natural theology" to justify one's faith; the argument from faith itself was now more powerful.

Among the aspects of Romanticism which contributed to this

appreciation of Christianity was its organic concept of human society. The eighteenth century had regarded society as being composed of atomistic individuals who joined together for reasons of self-interest. To the Romanticists, social organization was basic for individuality itself; societies had lives of their own, as living, growing things. This attitude encouraged greater respect for social institutions, among which were the churches. A concomitant of this attitude was a new appreciation of history, considered as the process by which organic societies had developed. The nineteenth century was an age of historicism, regarding Time as an essential element of any social process; Scott's historical novels and Ranke's scientific study of history were both symptoms of this attitude, which also produced a renewed interest in Biblical and church history. The antiquity and traditions of Christianity were treated with a new respect. In particular, there was a renewal of interest in the "ages of faith," the Middle Ages, which had hitherto been regarded as an unfortunate aberration in European history. In the eighteenth century, "Gothic" had been synonymous with "barbaric"; it was now regarded as something attractive, representative of a lost age of romance and harmony. (One aspect of this was the Gothic revival in architecture.) The new reverence for the past, and for the Middle Ages in particular, was especially helpful to the Roman Catholic Church, whose great ages were recalled with increased sympathy, and whose claims of unity and historic tradition had great appeal.

From the standpoint of religion, the most important element of Romanticism was its emphasis on the non-rational aspects of the human mind. It was characteristic of the Romantic era that it discussed the truth of religion in terms not of objective realities but of the subjective condition of the human personality. The new psychology, like the new history, opposed formal logic with the actual experience of man. The inner man, it was found, was a creature of instinct and sentiment. These instincts and sentiments were explored, not by empirical research, but by philosophical speculations, and these speculations produced the great contributions of the nineteenth century to theological thought in the form of the philosophy of religion.

The decisive impulse to this development was given by a philosopher of the late Enlightenment, Immanuel Kant, professor at the University of Königsberg (Kaliningrad). Kant's *Critique of Pure Reason* (1781) at once terminated the eighteenth-century debate on epistemology and commenced a revolution in philosophy. Kant transcended Lockeian empiricism, already devastated by Hume, by pointing out that the mind was not a passive recipient of sense-impressions; rather it organized and imposed order on the sensations it received. The mind had an inherent structure, independent of experience, which shaped thought according to *a priori* forms of perception and conception. On the other hand, Kant pointed out, the mind could only know that which is perceptible (*phenomena*) and could not deal with the reality of things-in-themselves (*noumena*). One consequence of this was that the ultimate truths of religion could not be demonstrated by reason. Kant's critical idealism thus provided a refuge from skepticism in the absolute laws of the mind, while at the same time demolishing the "natural theology" of the eighteenth-century apologists.

In the *Critique of Practical Reason* (1788) Kant provided a justification for religion to replace that which he had overthrown. Although pure reason cannot prove the ultimate truths of religion, there is the "practical reason"—the moral sense—innate in man, which demands belief in God, freedom and immortality. Morality, not reason, is the ground of faith. Kant, who had had a Pietistic upbringing, couched his conception of morality in rigid terms: the "categorical imperative" was "to act as if the maxim of our action were to become a universal law of nature." In his *Religion within the Limits of Pure Reason* (1793) Kant went further and argued that religious doctrines must be judged by their value for morality; the moral code is sovereign over churches and dogmas. Religious belief was vindicated by an appeal to the moral consciousness.

Kant commenced a philosophical revolution by turning man's interests from external sensations to the inner logic of the mind. Although his justification of religion was too subjective to be orthodox, he had opened up new lines of argument for belief which were both sounder and more powerful than "natural theology." By placing the grounds for belief in the moral consciousness, he had rendered it unassailable by rational arguments and had afforded the spokesmen of religion an opportunity to take the offensive against intellectual unbelief. By focusing philosophic interest on the inner state of the mind, Kant determined the direction of thought of the next generation of philosophers, most of whom were his disciples.

The greatest of these Idealists was G. W. F. Hegel, professor at the University of Berlin. Hegel differed from Kant on the question of the unknowability of *noumena*. The forms of the mind were identical with the forms of reality: "The real is rational, the rational real." The universe was explained as the working-out of the rational idea of the Absolute or World Spirit, which realizes itself through an evolutionary process, the "dialectical" movement of thesis, antithesis, and synthesis. History shows the working of the Spirit in the world, for it tells of the recurrent pattern of contradiction and resolution by which we progress to higher levels of consciousness. The Absolute was the highest self-consciousness, the ultimate resolution of diversity in unity. Religion was the expression of this principle in the form of myths. Christianity was the highest of religions, the most perfect figurative expression of the Absolute Idea.

The grandeur of Hegel's comprehensive vision more than made up for the obscurity of his terminology; for the generation after Kant he dominated German philosophy. He had, somewhat oddly, drawn conservative conclusions from his doctrines, treating the State as the present embodiment of the Spirit; hence his views received official favor. Perhaps his most lasting contribution was to have raised history to the dignity of philosophy, to have shown that reality was not static but a process of movement and change. From the religious standpoint, Hegel was significant for having provided a justification for the Christian religion as the figurative expression of philosophic reality. Such an apologetic has since been found incompatible with the orthodox Christian insistence on the absolute, not symbolic, truth of revelation; but it served in its time to place the revival of faith in one of the main streams of contemporary thought.

Even more influential than Hegel in religious philosophy was his contemporary and rival at Berlin, F. D. E. Schleiermacher, the most complete theologian of Romanticism. Schleiermacher made his reputation by his *Speeches on Religion to Its Cultured Despisers* (1799). He argued that religion was not a set of doctrinal propositions but rather a personal experience. The dogmas which the rationalists denied were merely provisional verbal formulations of the reality intuitively apprehended by "feeling" (religious experience). Religion was essentially a "feeling of absolute dependence" by which man directly apprehends God as the Being on whom he is dependent. Sin is the imperfect consciousness of God; redemption, the growing reawakening of that consciousness; Jesus Christ, the perfectly God-conscious man; the Holy Spirit, the consciousness of God acting through the Church, which is the community of believers.

Schleiermacher's great work, *The Christian Faith* (1821–1822), was perhaps the most influential theological writing of the century; his followers regarded it as a Protestant *Summa,* and it still provides many of the foundations of liberal theology. Schleiermacher's emphasis on personal religious experience as the foundation of faith, which was partly the fruit of his education among the Moravians, allowed him to go further than the rigid moralism of Kant in releasing religion from dependence on rational formulation; hence he was able to discard elements of theology which were contradicted by modern science and history. Another fruitful conception was his idea of the Church as the community of believers with a corporate experience of God and role in the process of redemption. These were ideas which were expanded upon by succeeding generations of theologians. On the other hand, Schleiermacher's doctrines have been subjected to severe criticism in his own day and since. Hegel was contemptuous of Schleiermacher's irrationalism; if religion was a feeling of dependence, he remarked caustically, the most religious animal was the dog. Others have accused Schleiermacher of pantheism, especially in his earlier works. Certainly his Christology cannot be described as orthodox. Yet in his unorthodoxy he succeeded, to a greater degree perhaps than any other theologian, in relating Christian faith to the leading trends of contemporary thought.

The Romantic philosophy of religion, exemplified by Kant, Hegel, and Schleiermacher, [2] was primarily a German product, but it had counterparts in other Protestant countries. The comparable movement in America was known as "transcendentalism." Another version was brought to England by Samuel Taylor Coleridge, better known as a Romantic poet, who had passed through various stages of revolt into a mature return to the Anglican Church. Coleridge was not entirely coherent in his re-affirmation of faith, and he borrowed an unfortunate terminology from the Germans, distinguishing "reason" (*Vernunft*) from "understanding" (*Verstehen*). The merely intellectual "understanding" deals only with the superficial world of sense, whereas the "reason" intuitively discerns the deeper spiritual realities. Faith was thus the perfection of intelligence, carrying it into a higher realm unattainable by rationalism. This concept of the higher reality of the spiritual world fortified many against the onslaughts of the utilitarian philosophers, notably Bentham and Mill, who were very influential in England.

The Romantic philosophers of religion had transmuted theology into philosophy. In the revival of orthodoxy which has characterized twentieth-century theology, their doctrines have been subjected to severe criticism. It can hardly be said that they presented a Christianity which was either orthodox or traditional. While the argument for religion generally had been strengthened, they had been less than successful in presenting an argument for Christianity specifically. Christianity claims a uniqueness for its revelation and an absoluteness for its basic dogmas which is ultimately incompatible with the treatment of them as mere symbols or stages in a generalized philosophy. Furthermore, the philosophic treatment of religion produced the-

---

2 Two other German philosophers whose Idealistic thought had relevance for the philosophy of religion were J. G. Fichte and Friedrich von Schelling.

ories of progress in terms of the growing self-realization of the Spirit or of the deeper God-consciousness of man, inducing an optimism which tended to disregard the elements of fear and agony which should not be ignored in Christian experience.

It is interesting to note that the neo-orthodox reaction of the twentieth century brought about a revival of the works of the most striking nineteenth-century opponent of the Romantic philosophers of religion, Søren Kierkegaard. Kierkegaard criticized Hegelianism for its detachment from the individual and his struggles, its disregard of the element of sin, and above all, its failure to acknowledge the absolute difference, the infinite abyss, between God and man. Christianity presented man not with syntheses but with contradictions and paradoxes, irreconcilable by reason. Salvation comes not through philosophic systems but by a personal commitment, born of despair, by which man takes the leap of faith into the realm of the absurd. This emphasis on decision and commitment has come to be known as "existentialism," a doctrine which properly belongs to the intellectual history of the twentieth rather than the nineteenth century. In his own day Kierkegaard had little influence, partly because he wrote in Danish and partly due to the eccentricity of his personality and ideas.

Whatever criticisms may be made of the Romantic philosophers of religion, it must be acknowledged that their justification of religious belief was admirably suited to the intellectual climate of the early nineteenth century. The alliance of religion with Romanticism was part of the general accommodation of the churches to the mood of reaction after the French Revolution. In various ways, men were seeking a principle of certainty, whether in objective authority or in subjective conviction. The revival of religion, the conservative reaction, and the Romantic critique of the Enlightenment coincided in a most timely fashion and reinforced each other. It seemed that the churches had won a decisive victory by their connection with the dominant tendencies of the post-revolutionary age; and for a generation this was indeed the case. In the long run, however, the close connection between the religious revival and the era of reaction was to prove of questionable benefit to the cause of religion. The mood of reaction provided insufficient positive principles for the guidance of society in an age which was to witness the most profound social and economic changes in European history. The fact that the revival of religion was so intimately linked with the doctrines and institutions of the post-revolutionary reaction provides the key to the varying fortunes of the churches in the nineteenth century.

6

The Roman Catholic Revival

In no church was the revival so impressive, or the connection with reaction so intimate, as in the Church of Rome. Purified by its sufferings during the Revolution, Roman Catholicism seemed to have shaken off many of the defects of past centuries and to have renewed its original inspiration. To an age in search of authority, it offered the principle and the institutions of authority; to an age which sought stability and certainty, it offered the example of steadfastness and the immutability of infallible dogma. Both reaction and romanticism contributed to make the decades after 1815 a period of revival for Roman Catholicism, which was regarded not only as a bulwark of the social order but as a source of creative inspiration. Basically conservative, the Church nonetheless produced several new movements which attempted to reconcile the Christian faith with the conditions of the modern world. Although many of these movements collapsed after clashing with ecclesiastical authority, the inner life of the Church went on with still greater vigor. The paradox of nineteenth-century religion was most clearly evident in the Roman Catholic Church, which came into more grievous intellectual and political conflict with the modern world than any other denomination, but which manifested at the same time a triumphantly persistent intensification of its devotional and institutional life.

In devotion and in discipline, the nineteenth century witnessed a Catholic renewal on a scale unparalleled since the high Middle Ages. In no previous century had so many new religious orders been founded. This was an index both of the revival of ecclesiastical life and of the need for extraordinary efforts to combat the de-Christianizing effects of the revolutionary age, for the vast majority of these orders were activist rather than contemplative.[1] The Society of Jesus, symbol of the vigor and intransigence of the Church, was revived in 1814 promptly upon the restoration of the Pope to Rome. The character of the secular clergy showed a gradual improvement, spiritual rather than intellectual, for which a model was provided by the saintly Curé of Ars, Jean Vianney. Among the laity, numerous pious societies indicated an increased participation in the life of the Church. In the field of ritual, a liturgical renewal began, associated with the name of Dom Prosper Guéranger, Abbot of Solesmes. Another characteristic of the inner life of the Church was the spread of popular devotions, particularly to the Sacred Heart, symbolizing the sufferings of Jesus on the Cross, and to the Virgin Mary, culminating in the definition of the dogma of the Immaculate Conception (1854)[2] and the reports of miracles at La Salette (1846) and Lourdes (1858). The most striking characteristic, however, of nineteenth-century Roman Catholicism was the renewed emphasis on the authority of the Pope, whose effective control over the Church reached its highest point.

Never since the Reformation had the Papacy been in so favor-

[1] Among the congregations of priests were two founded to counteract the de-Christianization of France after the Revolution: the Oblates of Mary Immaculate and the Society of Mary (Marists). The Salesians of Don Bosco were a teaching order which began in Turin as a response to urban destitution. The Marianists and the Congregation of the Holy Cross were teaching orders of priests and brothers. Another teaching order was the Brothers of Christian Instruction, founded by Lamennais' younger brother. Congregations of women were particularly numerous and were usually devoted to teaching or works of mercy.

[2] In the words of the Bull *Ineffabilis Deus:* "The most blessed Virgin Mary, in the first instant of her conception, by a singular grace and privilege granted by almighty God, in view of the merits of Jesus Christ, the Savior of the human race, was preserved free from all stain of original sin. . . ."

able a moral position as when Pius VII returned to Rome in 1814. Combining a conciliatory temper with a firm maintenance of his rights, Pius had won the respect of all Europe by his courageous resistance to Napoleon. The practical fruits of this situation were reaped by his Secretary of State, Consalvi, perhaps the ablest statesman produced by the Roman Curia. At the Congress of Vienna (1814–1815), Consalvi obtained the restoration of virtually the entire Papal States. The re-establishment of his temporal sovereignty seemed to be a great triumph for the Pope, assuring his independence from the secular states. In the long run, however, it was a mixed blessing. The Papacy had accepted a position as part of the state-system of Restoration Europe, which was about to be challenged by the rising forces of liberalism and nationalism. The Papal States could not be preserved without the support of the great powers, on whom the Popes were ultimately dependent for the maintenance of their political position.

In the era of Pius VII and Consalvi, the relations of the Papacy with the states of Europe were unusually cordial. It was the age of concordats, by which Consalvi hoped to restore the position of the Church in countries in which ecclesiastical institutions had been disarranged by the Revolution. The Napoleonic Concordat of 1801 had set the precedent. After an attempt to negotiate a new concordat broke down, the 1801 settlement was substantially retained in France by an agreement reached in 1819. New concordats were signed with Sardinia and Bavaria in 1817, with Naples in 1818, and with the Kingdom of the Netherlands (including Belgium) in 1827. Special arrangements were agreed upon with Prussia in 1821, and later with other German states, despite difficulties caused by the reshuffling of boundaries and the subjection of many Catholics to Protestant rulers. The alliance of throne and altar seemed to have replaced the old pattern of Church-State conflict.

Despite his opposition to revolution and his friendliness with the conservative monarchies, Pius VII was no blind reactionary. Although he restored the Index and Inquisition, he refrained from joining the "Holy Alliance" formed by the monarchs. On the suggestion of Consalvi, he reorganized the government of the Papal States in 1816, retaining many of the French administrative innovations. This moderate policy won for Consalvi the enmity of the more conservative party among the cardinals, known as the *zelanti*. On the death of Pius VII in 1823, Consalvi had to retire. The next Pope, Leo XII, was the choice of the *zelanti*.

The reign of Leo XII was marked by one great political triumph for the Church: the winning of Catholic emancipation in Great Britain. While the Roman Catholics of England and Scotland were not numerous, the majority of the people of Ireland were Catholic, maintaining their faith despite oppression in the seventeenth and eighteenth centuries. Many of the personal disabilities inflicted by the "penal laws" were repealed after 1778, but Roman Catholics remained ineligible for public office. The union of Ireland with Britain in 1801 seemed to set the seal on the subjection of the Irish Catholics. "No-Popery" was indeed a strong force in Protestant Britain. Nonetheless, the Irish Catholics won their political rights. Organized by the "Liberator" Daniel O'Connell into an effective political organization, the Catholic Association, the Irish were able, by the orderly display of their strength, to force the enactment of Catholic emancipation in 1829.

The example of Ireland was followed by Belgium. The Kingdom of the Netherlands formed in 1815 was an artificial union of Protestant Holland with Catholic Belgium. The terms of the union placed the Catholic and French-speaking areas at a disadvantage, and the situation was made worse by the autocratic government of the king. The result was the development of a Belgian nationalism which united both the Catholics and the secular liberals. In 1830 a revolution broke out as part of a general revolutionary crisis in Europe, and the independence of Belgium was recognized by the great powers in 1831. Belgium became a liberal constitutional monarchy, providing for freedom of worship and instruction. A system of public education satisfactory to the Church was established in 1842. Although the unstable alliance of Catholics and Liberals broke down after 1846, the fact of its existence had demonstrated that Catholicism could make a successful adjustment to the modern political situation.

The examples of Ireland and Belgium proved to be exceptional rather than typical. The liberal and nationalistic tendencies, which in these instances had served Catholic interests, elsewhere came into conflict with the Church in its more usual situation as a part of the established order. In Spain [3] and Portugal, where dynastic civil wars in the 1820's and 1830's developed into classic struggles between liberals and reactionaries, the liberals triumphed over the opposition of the Church and instituted anticlerical legislation. Similarly, in Switzerland, a civil war broke out in 1847 between the Protestant liberals and the Catholic cantons (the *Sonderbund*), ending in the victory of the liberals.

Liberalism was the ideal of the rising middle and professional classes. Its key point was the doctrine that governments should be held responsible to their citizens by means of a constitution, providing for parliamentary government and guaranteed rights, including freedom of religion. Liberalism drew its intellectual heritage from the Enlightenment and some phases of the French Revolution; it was rationalistic and secularistic in its outlook. It was far from radical: it repudiated the equalitarian concept of democracy and opposed socialism in the name of the rights of property. However, it rejected the principle of absolute authority whether in State or Church, and hence it was a revolutionary force on the Continent. Further, the liberals were allied with nationalistic movements which threatened the stability of the existing state system. Liberalism came into conflict with the Church because of its association with revolution, its tendency to erect a purely secularistic society, and its specific opposition to the claims of the Church in such matters as civil marriage and public education.

The reign of Gregory XVI (1831–1846) was marked by a direct confrontation between the Church and liberalism. A devout monk, Gregory was unprepared to sympathize with the new tendencies. His accession coincided with a revolution in the Papal

---

[3] Spain produced two notable Catholic thinkers: Juan Donoso Cortes, whose ideas were similar to those of de Maistre, and the philosopher Jaime Balmes.

States which forced him to appeal for aid to Austria, which, under the leadership of Prince von Metternich, was the bulwark of reaction in central Europe. Yet even Austria joined with other great powers in urging reforms in the government of the Papal States, particularly the giving of a greater role to laymen. A limited reform was enacted, but probably nothing short of full secular government would have satisfied the radical elements, and the growing movement for Italian nationhood was demanding the incorporation of the Papal States in a united Italy. Gregory could hardly accede to such demands. Under the influence of his pro-Austrian Secretary of State Lambruschini, he came to oppose not merely the liberal pressures upon the Papal States, but all liberal and nationalistic movements elsewhere. Thus, when the Catholic Poles revolted against an oppressive Russian government in 1831, Gregory condemned their insurrection on the grounds that the civil power, ordained by God, ought never to be resisted. Despite the fact that Tsar Nicholas I took advantage of the suppression of the Polish revolt to weaken the Roman Catholic Church in the Russian Empire, Gregory refused to countenance rebellion. The threat to the Pope's position as a sovereign prince in Italy made him the defender of established governments everywhere, regardless of the loss of popular support for the Church which such a policy might entail. In effect, the Pope had become the prisoner of his own sovereignty.

It is against this background that we must see the dramatic rise and fall of the Liberal Catholic movement, which began in France as an integral part of the Catholic revival. Félicité de Lamennais, whose *Essay on Indifference* had made him a leading spokesman of the Church, provided the impetus for a new departure. At this time he considered himself not only an Ultramontane but a royalist, seeing in the restored Bourbons the embodiment of the principle of authority. Under King Charles X (1824–1830) the official position of the Church seemed to be strengthened: the death penalty was enacted for sacrilege and a bishop was placed in charge of education. But the king's Catholicism was of the Gallican variety: the Church was to be subordinated to the Crown and to strengthen its authority. This doctrine was offensive to Lamennais, who emphasized the supremacy of the Pope over the monarchs; and when one of his books was condemned by a civil court for its criticism of the regime, he turned against the monarchy altogether. Sensing that the reactionary policies of Charles X were bound to lead to a revolution, Lamennais was determined that the Church should not be involved in the fall of the monarchy. In one bound he passed from legitimism to democracy, proposing to "baptize the Revolution." A latent democratic principle had, in fact, been inherent in his doctrine of the universal consensus of mankind as the basis of religious certainty. Catholicism, betrayed by the monarchs, was to place its trust in the people. The Church, seeking liberty for itself, must accept the principle of liberty for all.

The revolution of 1830, which overthrew the Bourbons, seemed to confirm at least part of Lamennais' judgment. Yet the revolution had been accompanied by attacks on churches, and the new king, Louis Philippe, was indifferent to religion. The government, although it allowed freedom of expression, did not permit the Church to set up schools free of secular control. Lamennais determined to employ the liberties already obtained to win the full freedom of the Church from a state which, in the hands of secular liberals, was effectively non-Christian. He was joined by a band of young men, of whom the most prominent were the priest Lacordaire and Comte Charles de Montalembert. They were encouraged by the successful union of Catholics and liberals in Ireland and Belgium. They founded a journal, *l'Avenir* ("the Future"), and an organization, the *Agence générale pour la défense de la liberté religieuse*. Their motto was "God and Liberty," and their goal was the separation of the Church from the state.

This program met opposition not only from the government but from the French bishops, still largely Gallican in their orientation. With characteristic but fatal boldness, Lamennais and his friends decided to suspend *l'Avenir* after a brilliant thirteen-month career and to appeal their cause directly to the Pope. Naively confident that their Ultramontanism outweighed their liberalism, the "pilgrims of God and of liberty" arrived in Rome at the beginning of 1832. Gregory XVI, however, was not the man to sympathize with their liberal program, and the direct appeal to the Pope only precipitated the condemnation of their doctrines. The encyclical *Mirari vos* (August 1832) denounced the error of "indifferentism" with its corollaries: freedom of conscience, of speech and of the press, and the separation of Church and state. It was a clear condemnation of the program of the Liberal Catholics, They submitted and terminated *l'Avenir* and the *Agence générale*. But Lamennais, sensitive and passionate, had suffered a shattering blow. His whole system rested on the authority of the Pope, which had now been turned against him. The very exaggeration of his doctrines proved fatal to his faith. In 1834 he published *Paroles d'un Croyant,* a passionate declaration of his democratic principles. Again he was condemned, this time explicitly, by the encyclical *Singulari nos.* Lamennais left the Church, never to return.

The fall of Lamennais did not result in the undoing of his work. His earlier writings had dealt a blow to Gallicanism from which it never recovered; the next generation of French Catholics, whether liberal or reactionary, was thoroughly Ultramontane. Lamennais carried no one with him in his fall, and his disciples became the ablest defenders of Catholicism in France. The submission of Montalembert and Lacordaire was sincere, but it did not entail the abandonment of the hope of refashioning Catholic life in conformity with the political situation of the age of liberalism. Warned by the experience of 1832, the Liberal Catholics avoided general principles and devoted themselves to practical activities. Lacordaire continued the Catholic revival with his lectures at Nôtre Dame and refounded the Dominican Order in France. Another leader, Frédéric Ozanam, founded the Society of St. Vincent de Paul to engage in work among the poor.

In 1842, Montalembert organized a Catholic political party. The issue was that of freedom of instruction for religious bodies, guaranteed by the constitution but denied in practice. As elsewhere in Europe, the conflict of religious versus secular education was the one issue on which devout Catholics could reach political agreement. By resting his argument on liberal constitutional grounds, Montalembert was able to unite the Catholics behind a cry for liberty. It was an opportunistic policy, more moderate than that of *l'Avenir:* Montalembert had never really been a democrat, and he no longer sought separation of Church and state. But by forming a Catholic party on liberal grounds he had achieved the aim of *l'Avenir,* of a Catholicism in harmony with modern ideals, seeking liberty for the nation as well as itself. When the next revolution occurred in France in 1848, the Church was among the victors, not the victims.

A parallel movement of Catholic revival, also tending in a liberal direction, took place in Germany. What made German Catholicism unique was the fact that in Germany, as nowhere else on the Continent, Catholics lived in direct proximity to Protestants. They could not avoid the currents of modern thought which largely emanated from Protestant sources; at the same time, they were forced into a greater awareness of their identity as a religious group. The result was a liveliness and variety of expression which might have been stifled in more homogeneously Catholic countries.

It was a Church-State conflict which first made the German Catholics aware of the necessity of acting as a body. Germany was divided into thirty-nine sovereign states, most of which were ruled by Protestants. In the largest state, Prussia, there were substantial Catholic minorities, especially in the Rhineland and the Polish provinces. In 1837 a controversy broke out over the issue of mixed marriages. Prussian law required that children should be reared in the religion of the father; the Roman Catholic hierarchy insisted on a Catholic upbringing for all children with any Catholic parent. The Prussian government imprisoned the Archbishops of Cologne and Posen. Only in 1840, after the accession of a new king, was the issue resolved in favor of the Catholic position. The resulting upsurge of Catholic feeling was channeled into political action. In 1848 national meetings of Catholic bishops and laymen were held, a practice which later developed into the annual *Katholikentagen*. The Prussian Catholics combined for electoral purposes, forming a group of deputies in the Diet who were later known as the "Center" Party.

The central issues in German Catholicism were, however, not political but intellectual. Constant intercourse with their Protestant neighbors had forced German Catholics to become familiar with the arguments of the enemies of the Church and to realize the insufficiency of the conventional Catholic apologetic. Sometimes, in the effort to justify the position of the Church in modern philosophic terms, German Catholic philosophers found it difficult to stay within the limits of doctrinal orthodoxy. Franz von Baader sought to combine mysticism with critical philosophy; his doctrines of the interpenetration of faith and knowledge were not entirely orthodox. A theologian, Georg Hermes, developed a rationalistic presentation of the Catholic faith which, although intended to oppose the doctrines of Kant, was much influenced by them. The Hermesian doctrine was condemned in 1835–1836. Similarly, Anton Günther, seeking to counteract the pantheism implicit in Hegelian philosophy, fell under the spell of his opponent, and his books were placed on the Index in 1857.

The most successful German presentations of the Roman Catholic position took the form, not of philosophic speculations, but of historical research. This was an opportune field in which to compete with Protestants, since the nineteenth century was dominated by the historical or developmental approach, and the Romantic rediscovery of the Middle Ages gave to the great period of Catholic history a new significance.[4] The critical approach to history had been largely pioneered by Protestants, but German Catholic scholars mastered both the techniques and the spirit of historicism. The first center of their historical studies was the University of Tübingen, where the Catholic theological faculty existed side by side with a Protestant faculty which was famous for its historical work. The Catholic Tübingen school emphasized the organic development of Christianity and sought,

---

[4] The Romantic movement led to several conversions to Roman Catholicism, notably Friedrich von Schlegel in 1808.

in the manner of their Protestant colleagues, to reconstruct theology on an historical foundation. In their enforced competition, it was necessary for Catholics to match Protestants in scholarly objectivity, trusting only to historical truth for the protection of religious doctrines. Yet their objectivity concealed an apologetic purpose: the demonstration that the Roman Catholic faith could withstand historical scrutiny was in itself a refutation of many of the most severe Protestant attacks.

The greatest Catholic scholar produced by Tübingen was Johann Adam Möhler. His *Symbolik* (1832), a study of the Catholic and Protestant creeds, examined the traditions of the Church to demonstrate the necessity of the primacy of the Pope. Late in life Möhler accepted a chair at the University of Munich, where the professor of ecclesiastical history was Johann Joseph Görres, a former rationalist turned Catholic apologist. Görres' great work on *Christian Mysticism* (1838–1842) was a learned historical study which sought to demonstrate the reasonableness of faith in the supernatural. With the coming of Görres and Möhler, Munich, the capital of Catholic Bavaria, became the center of German Catholic intellectual life.

The most distinguished scholar of the Munich school was Ignaz von Döllinger, the greatest and most tragic figure of Liberal Catholicism after Lamennais. A priest, Döllinger turned to history as the best defense of the Church. With the four volumes of his *Church History* (1833–1838) and his work on the *Reformation* (1848), he became the accepted spokesman of Roman Catholicism among historians. Döllinger regarded Christianity as the product of history rather than of philosophy; in him, historicism reached to the heart of theology itself. Scientific history, he felt, would serve the Church better than scholasticism. Such an approach tended to an intellectual liberalism, although in politics Döllinger was a conservative. He asserted that freedom was necessary for the operation of the Church and that Catholics must claim this freedom for others as well as themselves. The liberal tendency of his views was restrained by his innate conservatism and his practical services to the Church. Until the 1860's, Döllinger was regarded as a faithful spokesman of German Catholicism who had demonstrated that scholarly research could be an ally, rather than an enemy, of the faith. Under his leadership, Germany produced an indigenous form of Liberal Catholicism, historical rather than political in its emphasis.

One other country in which a Liberal Catholic tendency emerged was Italy, the center of the Roman Catholic world. Here the Church was most directly confronted with the problem of nationalism. Italy was not a nation—Metternich called it a mere "geographical expression"—but was split up into a number of principalities, largely dominated by the power of the Austrian Empire, which included two provinces in the north. Of the other states, the Bourbon kingdom of Naples and Sicily was perhaps the most rotten monarchy in Europe; the Papal States lay athwart the center of the peninsula; the other central Italian principalities were Austrian puppets; and the kingdom of Sardinia, whose strength was in the northeastern province of Piedmont, was to become the focus of liberal and nationalistic activities. A growing nationalist movement sought the unification, or at least the federation, of the peninsula; but there were several problems which had first to be faced: Was united Italy to be a monarchy or a republic? Which state was to lead it? How was the unpopular alien rule of Austria to be eliminated? And, finally, what was to be done with the temporal power of the Pope in central Italy? The last problem was to prove the most difficult. The Pope's place was in Rome, of which he was bishop as well as prince; yet he could not, in view of his supranational role as head of the Church, accept a position either as ruler or as a subject of a national state. Italy could neither live with nor without the Pope.

The most radical solution was also the most threatening to the Pope: the complete unification of Italy, with the consequent abolition of the Papal States. None of the princely states was yet ready to undertake such a program. The leading proponents of unification were therefore the republicans—the most advanced revolutionaries. Repressed by the governments and shunned by respectable society, the revolutionaries organized themselves into secret societies, of which the *Carbonari* were the most famous. All their revolts proved abortive, but they contributed to the state of tension which had turned Gregory XVI so strongly against liberalism. Out of the welter of conspiracies emerged the greatest prophet of nationalism, Giuseppe Mazzini, whose writings invested duty to the nation with the sanctity of a religious cause. His ideas were unacceptable to the Church, for he substituted for Christianity a pantheistic religion of humanity.

A more Catholic solution was proposed by a Piedmontese priest, Vincenzo Gioberti. In his *Moral and Civil Primacy of the Italians* (1843), Gioberti urged a rebirth of the ancient greatness of Italy under the auspices of the Church. Italy should be a federation of principalities under the presidency of the Pope. Antonio Rosmini-Serbati, the founder of a religious order, the Institute of Charity, was also a proponent of the national cause in harmony with the Papacy. In his *Five Wounds of the Holy Church* (1848), Rosmini dealt boldly with defects in the structure of the Church itself.

These reformers met with no sympathy from the regime of Gregory XVI. To complicate matters, both Rosmini and Gioberti engaged in philosophical speculations which resulted in attacks upon their orthodoxy. Both were inclined toward a philosophy of ontologism which maintained that the primary operation of the intellect is a direct intuition of "being," identified with God. They were opposed by the rising influence of the Jesuits, who were politically reactionary and philosophically committed to scholasticism; eventually various writings of Gioberti and Rosmini were condemned.

In France, Germany, and Italy, the Catholic revival, which had begun as part of a general trend of post-revolutionary reaction, had turned significantly in a liberal direction. A movement of Liberal Catholicism had begun, exalting the Pope and the Church but calling upon them to make an adjustment to the political and intellectual conditions of the modern world. These Liberal Catholics were the most effective spokesmen of the Roman Catholic faith in their day, for they recognized that the Church must make its way in an alienated society, and they spoke to that society in its own language. In so doing, they expressed thoughts which were uncongenial to traditional Catholicism and frequently incompatible with it. The more effectively they spoke to the nineteenth century, the more they came under the suspicions of the authorities of the Church. Roman Catholicism had, since the Reformation, behaved as if in a "state of siege," under constant attack by a hostile world. The Catholic revival of the early nineteenth century opened up an opportunity to break out of the siege. The fortress mentality, however, was still strong, especially in the entirely Catholic countries of southern Europe. The Papacy, on which all depended, seemed to have chained itself to the established order by the golden fetters of the temporal power. At mid-century, the stage was set for a confrontation of the old and the new viewpoints.

7

Pius IX: Catholicism Versus Liberalism

The death of Pope Gregory XVI virtually coincided with one of the great revolutionary moments in European history, the revolution of 1848, in which the forces of liberalism had their best opportunity to shape the destiny of Europe. It was also a moment of opportunity for the Church to break out of the mold of unalterable hostility to the leading tendencies of the modern world. Neither of these opportunities was realized; instead, 1848 proved to be the "turning point on which history failed to turn." After a brief revival of the hopes of Liberal Catholicism, the Papacy resumed its conflict with liberalism and nationalism, a conflict in which the Church suffered grievous external losses but achieved internal consolidation. The reign of Pius IX (1846–1878), the longest in the history of the Church, witnessed the abasement of the Papacy in the temporal sphere and the greatest extension of its authority in the spiritual.

The reign of Pius IX (called Pio Nono in Italian) began with the highest of hopes for a more liberal Church. The Conclave of 1846 was marked by a reaction against the *zelanti* and Austrian influence. It elected Cardinal Mastai-Ferretti, who was known to be benevolent and open-minded and was reputed to be "liberal." His "liberalism" consisted of a desire to please his subjects and a vague pro-Italian, anti-Austrian political outlook. His first actions tended to confirm the impression of liberalism. He granted an amnesty to political prisoners, fostered economic improvements in the Papal States, instituted a citizen militia, successfully opposed an Austrian attempt to occupy the city of Ferrara, and, late in 1847, established an elective consultative assembly and a council of ministers which included laymen. These acts were only tentative steps towards the liberal ideal, and perhaps Pius did not wish to go further; but he had created the image of the "liberal Pope" which made him a popular hero and the hope of Italian nationalism.

Still more was expected of him. When a wave of revolutions broke out in Europe early in 1848, Pius had to grant a liberal constitution with a ministry responsible to an elected parliament. Efforts were then made to draw the Pope—who had uttered the cry "Lord God, bless Italy!"—into a war with Austria upon which the Italian nationalists, led by the King of Sardinia, had staked their cause. Had Pius taken this step, he could have assumed the leadership of a united Italy, but he would have betrayed his obligations as head of the Church. The position of the Pope as a temporal constitutional monarch was a false one. His lay ministers might enact measures which, as a religious leader, he condemned; and the state of which he was sovereign might find itself at war with a nation such as Catholic Austria with which, as universal Pontiff, he had to maintain friendly relations. At the end of April, 1848, Pius announced his refusal to join in the war against Austria. This was the decisive act which separated him from the nationalist cause.

The immediate effect was a popular disillusionment which weakened the Pope's position in Rome itself. The extreme democratic party, influenced by the republicanism of Mazzini, grew stronger. The Pope's most capable minister, Rossi, was assassinated. Threatened by mob violence, Pius fled from Rome on November 24 to Gaeta in the kingdom of Naples. The Mazzinians took over Rome, deposed the Pope, and formed a republic, while Pius appealed to the powers of Europe to restore him to his temporal states. His appeal coincided with a general reversal of the tide of revolution: by 1849 conservative forces were again in control in most states of Europe. As part of this process, a French army crushed the Roman revolution in 1849, and in 1850

Pius returned as sovereign to his capital. He was thoroughly disillusioned with his experiment in moderate liberalism, and his new Secretary of State, Cardinal Antonelli, reinstituted the absolutist regime. The liberal Pope had joined the counter-revolution.

In France, too, the hopes of Liberal Catholicism were first raised and then dashed. The Revolution of 1848 brought forth a conservative Republic in which the Catholic party led by Montalembert held a leading position. The Church was shown full respect during the Revolution; bishops and priests were elected to the Chamber; and Lacordaire briefly took his seat on the extreme Left, although he soon had to resign. The crushing of a revolt of the Parisian workers brought an alliance of all the moderate and conservative groups in the defense of order and property. Louis Napoleon, nephew of the late emperor, was elected President and posed as the savior of civil order and the Church. A French army was sent to Rome to restore the Pope, and Montalembert's friend, the Comte de Falloux, was made Minister of Education and Public Worship. In this position he was able to achieve the goal for which the Catholic party had been organized, the freedom of Catholic education. The Falloux Law of 1850, a compromise with the moderate liberals, allowed the Church freely to establish primary and secondary schools, although the state-controlled University kept the monopoly of higher degrees. A second part of the law allowed bishops and priests a degree of influence even in the management of the secular schools, with the result that public education was weakened relatively to the Church's school system. This has caused the Falloux Law to be regarded by historians as a triumph of clericalism, although in fact it was a victory for the Catholic liberals.

It was a victory which resulted in a split in the Catholic party. An intransigent faction led by Louis Veuillot, editor of *l'Univers,* objected to the concessions to the liberals which Falloux had made. Veuillot, an able but virulent journalist, aggressively asserted the fullest claims of the Church, abandoning the ideal of political liberty which Montalembert still maintained. Veuillot carried the debate beyond politics into the internal affairs of the Church, arguing for the complete authority and infallibility of the Pope and for a thorough opposition to the spirit of the modern world. The school of Montalembert, whose organ was *le Correspondant,* insisted that "not everything in the modern spirit is bad"; but their cause was ruined by their political policy. In 1852, after a coup d'état, Louis Napoleon proclaimed himself Emperor as Napoleon III. Veuillot, regarding Napoleon as the protector of the Pope, supported him fully, while Montalembert opposed his suppression of liberty. A majority of the French Catholics joined Veuillot in supporting Napoleon as the defender of order and religion; they had come to identify Catholicism with the defense of the bourgeois society. Montalembert and his friends were nearly isolated, while Veuillot, backed by the Pope, appeared as the voice of French Catholicism.

Catholics now found themselves divided into two factions, Liberal and Ultramontane. The term "Ultramontane" had originally designated the entire movement of Catholic revival, with its emphasis on papal authority. Now that Pius IX had been forced into a position of reaction, "Ultramontane" came to designate the clericalist group which favored his policy of regarding the Church as being in a "state of siege," opposed to the ruling tendencies of the age, isolated and militant. Similarly the term "Liberal Catholic," which had originally designated all those who had been stirred into activity by the vision of Lamennais, came to have a more restricted meaning, indicating those who clung to the hopes of a reconciliation of Catholicism with liberal society even when such hopes were disapproved by the authorities of the Church. The fact that Church authority after 1850 committed itself to the more reactionary position was decisive for the great mass of Catholics. The Liberal Catholic movement, however brilliant its leaders and however attractive its dreams, was always the movement of a minority.

The division which was thus manifested in France extended itself to other countries. In Germany, the Munich school led by Döllinger came to be challenged by the school of Mainz, which emphasized the immediate authority of the Pope as against the independence claimed by scientific and historical research. In England, a Liberal Catholic group was formed, led by Döllinger's

disciple, Sir John (later Lord) Acton, and a convert from Anglicanism, Richard Simpson, who expressed their views in two able
magazines, the *Rambler* and later the *Home and Foreign Review*. However, this group met increasing opposition from the
hierarchy, and it never obtained the full support of the outstanding figure of English Catholicism, the leader of the converts,
John Henry Newman. An index of the degree to which the Lib-
eral-Ultramontane split had excited the tempers of Catholics is
the fact that the moderate and judicious Newman, always submissive to authority, was regarded with suspicion as a dangerous
liberal by many both in England and in Rome. The division of
the Catholics into Ultramontanes and Liberals prevented the full
employment of their resources in a critical period.

These years, however, were not without triumphs for the
Church. In England, the fruits of emancipation were beginning
to be reaped. Converts from the Oxford Movement in the
Church of England began to come over after 1845, and an extensive immigration from Ireland after the Great Famine vastly increased the numbers of Catholics in England, which could no
longer be regarded as an outlying mission of the Church. In 1850
Pius IX established in England a full hierarchy, headed by Nicholas Cardinal Wiseman as Archbishop of Westminster. This so-
called "Papal aggression" led to an outburst of Protestant protest
which, however, had no practical effect. Despite a series of internal quarrels between the hereditary Catholics and the converts,
English Catholicism began a steady growth. Similarly, the growth
of Roman Catholicism in Holland was recognized by the establishment of a hierarchy in that country in 1853. A concordat was
signed with Austria in 1855, on terms very favorable to the
Church. In 1854, by defining the dogma of the Immaculate Conception, Pius IX demonstrated the extent of his claims and the
fullness of his authority within the Church.

Indeed, as the external position of the Papacy came to be
increasingly threatened in this period, the internal authority of
the Papacy was increased. The Pope himself came to be the object of personal affection and devotion among Catholics. Neither
an adept statesman nor a trained intellectual, Pio Nono was an

exemplary priest with a most attractive personality, and his political misfortunes only enhanced his popularity.

The political situation of Europe was the source of the misfortunes of Pius IX. He was blind to the power of the liberal ideal, which was forcing a readjustment of the relation of the Church to secular society, and he missed the opportunity to achieve a suitable compromise. There were, indeed, excessively secularistic elements in the liberal movement to which no Catholic could give his approval; but there were also moderates with whom compromise would have been possible had they not been alienated by a policy of intransigence. The fatal obstacle to compromise was the temporal power of the Pope in the States of the Church, which Pius regarded as an inalienable heritage of the Papacy which he was committed to defend. The movement for Italian unification (the *risorgimento*) had been checked but not crushed in 1848; it was renewed in the 1850's and threatened to despoil the Pope of his temporal sovereignty.

The leadership of the Italian cause fell to the kingdom of Sardinia (Piedmont), the only state in the peninsula with a liberal constitution, whose Prime Minister from 1852 was one of the greatest statesmen of the century, Camillo di Cavour. Cavour sought to unite all or most of Italy under the Sardinian monarchy, thus achieving the goals of nationalism without recourse to Mazzinian republicanism. He won the support of the radicals by enacting anti-clerical legislation in 1852 and 1855, which abolished contemplative religious orders and redistributed the property of the Church, over the protests of the hierarchy. Such actions raised the prospect of the spoliation of the Church, in the event that the Papal States fell into Piedmontese hands. This was later to be one of the obstacles to a compromise between Pius and Cavour. However, Italian propagandists succeeded in awakening much sympathy for the Piedmontese cause in other countries, and in 1858 Napoleon III agreed to an alliance with Sardinia to drive the Austrians out of Italy.

The first act in the *risorgimento* opened with the war of 1859, in which the Franco-Sardinian forces defeated the Austrian army. Fearing that his Italian ally would become too powerful, Napo-

leon suddenly concluded an armistice with Austria by which
Sardinia was to receive only one Austrian province. Events, however, had moved too rapidly. The liberals in the central Italian
states (Tuscany, Modena, and Parma) revolted, deposed their
rulers, and demanded annexation to Sardinia. They were joined
by the population of the northernmost province of the Papal
States, the Romagna. This province, the furthest from Rome,
had always been the most turbulent; only the Austrian armies
had held it down. Napoleon, who posed as the protector of the
Church, had hoped to prevent these revolts by his sudden armistice; but now, confronted with the *fait accompli,* he changed his
position. Early in 1860 he agreed to allow the annexation of
central Italy, including the Romagna, to the kingdom of Sardinia. The Pope had been despoiled of one of the States of the
Church.

Cavour had succeeded in expanding Sardinia into a kingdom
of north Italy. Perhaps he did not intend to go further; but he
had done enough to alarm devout Catholics throughout Europe.
A small international army was formed to defend what remained
of the Papal States. Because of his agreement with Cavour, Napoleon III lost the support of the Catholic party in France: Veuillot
and Montalembert joined in denouncing his policy. Catholics in
other countries gave testimonials of their indignation at the
spoliation of the Papal States and urged their governments to
come to the aid of the Pope. It was in vain.

In the spring of 1860, a band of Mazzinians, led by Giuseppe
Garibaldi, left from a Piedmontese port for Sicily. By bluff and
daring, they quickly won control of the island, crossed to the
mainland, and easily captured Naples. It appeared that Garibaldi
was ready to proclaim a radical republic in south Italy and even
march on Rome. This was more than Cavour had bargained for:
he distrusted Garibaldi's radicalism, and an attack on Rome
might force Napoleon III, anxious to conciliate the French Catholics, back to his role as protector of the Church. To halt Garibaldi, Cavour decided to send the Sardinian army into Naples.
Unfortunately, the States of the Church were in the army's path.
The Sardinians were met by the motley Papal army, easily de-

UNIFICATION OF ITALY

SWITZERLAND

To
France
(1860)

A U S T R I A N   E M P I R E

PIEDMONT

Turin

LOMBARDY
1859
Milan

VENETIA
1866

Venice

FRANCE

To
France

PARMA
1860

MODENA
1860

Ferrara

ROMAGNA
1860

TURKISH

EMPIRE

Florence

TUSCANY
1860

MARCHES
1861

UMBRIA
1861

CORSICA
(Fr.)

PATRIMONY
Rome
1870

NAPLES
1861

Naples

SARDINIA

K G D M.   O F   S A R D I N I A

P A P A L   S T A T E S

K G D M.   O F   T H E   T W O   S I C I L I E S

—— Boundary of states (1859)

---- Boundary of provinces

1860 Date of annexation by Sardinia (Italy)

SICILY
1861

feated it, and occupied the provinces of Umbria and the Marches, leaving to the Papacy only the area immediately around Rome, the "Patrimony of St. Peter." This was the second stage in the elimination of the Papal States. Cavour's forces, to whom Garibaldi yielded his conquests, then occupied the rest of south Italy. Annexation to Sardinia was approved by plebiscites. Except for the vicinity of Rome, Italy was virtually united, and the King of Sardinia, Victor Emmanuel II, took the title of King of Italy in 1861.

Pius IX denounced those who had despoiled him and excommunicated Victor Emmanuel. Cavour, whose motto was "a free Church in a free State," made overtures to reconcile the Papacy to the kingdom of Italy, but his reputation for anti-clericalism discouraged trust in him, and in June, 1861, he suddenly died. He had unified Italy but had not stabilized the new regime. His successors were restrained from seizing Rome only by the presence of a French army. Pius, however, could not rely on his French protector. Napoleon III, anxious to disengage himself from his Italian entanglements, actually agreed in 1864 to evacuate his troops from Rome, but a Garibaldian attack on the city in 1867 brought them back. For the defense of his temporal sovereignty, the Pope was dependent upon foreign arms.

The "Roman question," the issue of the temporal power of the Papacy, became the dominant issue in the history of the Church for over a decade. The ideal solution, no doubt, would have been the cession of the temporal power—an embarrassment rather than a source of strength to the Pope—in return for an effective guarantee of the independence of the Papacy, such as was arranged in 1929. However, Pius IX could not accept such a solution, partly because of the past history of Sardinian aggression, but also because he felt himself personally obligated to maintain unimpaired the heritage of the Church which he had received. The ideal of the "free Church in a free State" was a liberal ideal with apparently secularistic connotations; and behind liberalism Pius saw the spectre of revolution led by still more radical elements. He determined upon a course of intransigence, drawing Catholicism in upon itself and presenting a solid front of resistance to a hostile world. The Roman Catholic Church came to regard itself as in a "state of siege," and it adopted the hard, militant mentality appropriate to that condition. It is in this period that the word "Ultramontanism" came to have its ultimate meaning of thoroughgoing resistance to the dominant tendencies of the modern world.

A by-product of this state of tension among Catholics was the final defeat of the Liberal Catholic movement. The Ultramontane outlook, stressing dependence on Rome and suspicion of modern ideas, dominated both the hierarchy and the Catholic masses. Its advocates were led in France by Veuillot, in Ireland by Paul Cullen, Archbishop of Dublin, and in England by the converts W. G. Ward, editor of the *Dublin Review*, Frederick Faber, a noted hymnologist, and Henry Edward Manning, who became Archbishop of Westminster in 1865. Men such as Montalembert, Döllinger, and Acton came under increasing suspicion and, in turn, tended toward more liberal positions which further alienated them from the sympathies of most Catholics. In 1863, Montalembert, addressing the Belgian Catholics at Malines, espoused the ideal of a "free Church in a free State" and demanded liberty of conscience. The Jesuit editor of the Roman journal *Civiltà Cattolica* attempted to justify Montalembert's speech by drawing a distinction between the "thesis," the full claims of the Church, and the "hypothesis," the practical adjustment to the necessities of the actual situation. Pope Pius, much disturbed by this, expressed his displeasure privately. In the same year, Döllinger, presiding over a congress of German scholars at Munich, demanded the replacement of scholasticism by historical research conducted with perfect freedom. He was rebuked by a Papal letter to the Archbishop of Munich, early in 1864, which insisted that scholarly research must be subordinated to ecclesiastical authority. The condemnation of freedom of scholarship was so clear that Acton in England felt obliged to put an end to his periodical, the *Home and Foreign Review*.

The reign of Pius IX saw the fullest exposition and exercise of the authority of the Pope and was more prolific of doctrinal statements and condemnations than any since the Counter-

Reformation. The various condemnations of "the principal errors of our times" issued by Pius were gathered together in one
document, the famous *Syllabus of Errors,* appended to the encyclical *Quanta cura* in 1864. The encyclical condemned the idea
that society should be governed without regard to religion and
censured the Liberal Catholic doctrine that assent may be with-
held from those Papal decisions which did not deal with dogmas
of faith or morals. The *Syllabus* was a list of eighty propositions
which had been condemned in previous Papal utterances. While
many of the condemned propositions were obviously anti-Christian, the *Syllabus* attracted attention by its condemnation of
liberal doctrines concerning the political rights of the Church,
civil marriage, the separation of Church and State, liberty of
thought and religion, and the position of the Pope. It concluded
by condemning the proposition that "the Roman Pontiff can and
ought to reconcile himself and come to terms with progress, liberalism and modern civilization."

To most readers, unacquainted with the technical language of
Roman documents,[1] it seemed as if the Pope had declared war
on the nineteenth century. The position of the Liberal Catholics,
who had hoped for a reconciliation of Roman Catholicism with
liberal society, was clearly untenable; and even many moderates
were stunned by the sweeping condemnations, while the extreme
Ultramontanes rejoiced. Balance was restored to the situation by

[1] The *Syllabus,* designed for the use of bishops, was drawn up in technical
theological language and was unsuited for public dissemination. It consists
of a list, compiled by Cardinal Antonelli as Secretary of State, of eighty condemned propositions, to each of which is appended a citation of the Papal
document in which it was condemned. Thus the condemnations cannot be
understood by themselves, without reference to the original sources (encyclicals, allocutions, and letters) from which they derive whatever force they
possess. In their original form they were generally of specific and limited
application. Thus the final proposition, so extreme when quoted by itself, is
taken from the allocution *Jamdudum cernimus* (1861) which, criticizing
political liberalism as manifested in Italy, denied that "the Roman Pontiff
should reconcile himself and come to terms with *what they call* progress,
Liberalism, and recent civilization." Much of the apparent harshness of Papal
documents results from the process by which statements such as this are reduced to abstract propositions asserted or condemned in universal terms.

a brilliant pamphlet published by the liberal Bishop Dupanloup of Orléans, who "minimized" the offense given by the *Syllabus* by placing the condemned propositions in their proper context. Dupanloup made use of the distinction between thesis and hypothesis, pointing out that the *Syllabus* dealt with absolute propositions, while the Church often allowed practical adjustments to the actual state of society. Dupanloup's interpretation was generally accepted among Catholics. However, no amount of minimization could disguise the fact that the *Syllabus* was, if not a complete condemnation of modern society, certainly a sign of unchanged opposition to the trend of liberalism on the Continent.

The leading tendencies of the reign of Pius IX—hostility to liberalism, the dominance of Ultramontanism, and the growth of the power and prestige of the Pope within the Church—reached their consummation with the first Vatican Council, which Pius summoned to meet in December, 1869. The most important proposal brought before this ecumenical council was the definition of the dogma of Papal Infallibility. The Ultramontanes, some of whom had gone to extreme lengths in their adoration of the Pope, pressed for this definition, which would effectively condemn old-fashioned Gallicanism and symbolically reassert the Church's defiance of liberalism. The surviving Liberal Catholics, led by Döllinger and Acton, feared—erroneously as it proved—that a declaration of Infallibility would lead to the dogmatization of the *Syllabus* and of the necessity of the temporal power; and they organized an opposition among the bishops at the Council. The opposition, however, was hopelessly in a minority. An overwhelming majority approved the definition, which was proclaimed on July 18, 1870:

> that the Roman Pontiff, when he speaks *ex cathedra*, that is, when, exercising the office of pastor and teacher of all Christians, he defines by virtue of his supreme apostolic authority a doctrine concerning faith and morals to be held by the universal Church, through the divine assistance promised to him in St. Peter, is possessed of that infallibility with which the divine Redeemer willed that his Church be endowed in defining doctrine concerning faith and morals; and therefore, such definitions of the

Roman Pontiff are irreformable, of themselves and not from the consent of the Church.

The definition of Papal Infallibility marked the high point of the reign of Pius IX. It seemed to mark, also, the definitive victory of the Ultramontane party, even though the actual wording of the definition was more moderate than many of them had desired, and the authority thus attributed to the Pope has been, in practice, sparingly used. The Council terminated ingloriously the career of the Liberal Catholic movement, which was left with the alternatives of silence or schism. Döllinger refused to accept the dogma, which he regarded as a deviation from the tradition of the Church, and he was excommunicated in 1871. A group of his followers in Germany and Switzerland organized an "Old Catholic" Church, asserting that those who accepted infallibility were schismatics. However, the Old Catholics were few in number; drawn largely from the academic world, they were repudiated by an overwhelming majority of Roman Catholics. Outside the German lands, very few left the Church over the issue. All the bishops of the minority quickly proclaimed their submission.

The greatest triumph of Pius IX was almost immediately followed by his greatest defeat. Three days before the dogma of Papal Infallibility was proclaimed, war broke out between France and Prussia, resulting in the defeat and deposition of Napoleon III. As a consequence of the war, the French garrison had to be withdrawn from Rome. The Papal city was now defenseless, and the troops of the Kingdom of Italy occupied Rome on September 20, 1870. The temporal power of the Pope—the cause for which so much had been staked—had fallen.

The loss of his temporal sovereignty did not result, as had been feared, in any infringement of the liberty of the Pope as head of the Roman Catholic Church. The Italian government passed a Law of Guarantees which allowed the Pope to retain his personal status as a sovereign and the use of the Papal palaces, offered him a substantial pension, and abandoned most of the control of the state over the Church in Italy except for a redistribution of ecclesiastical property and income. It was a fair approximation of the "free Church in a free State" except for the defect that it was only a law, enacted unilaterally by the Italian government, and not a treaty, since the Pope would not consent to any agreement which acquiesced in the spoliation of his territory. Pius insisted that he was, in effect, a prisoner in the Vatican, and he refused to acknowledge the new regime. The result was a curious situation in which the Pope enjoyed the benefits of the Law of Guarantees, except for the pension which Pius spurned, but continued to maintain his claim to the Papal States, as did his successors until the Lateran Concordat of 1929.

Although Italy had been united, the refusal of the Papacy to come to terms with the new nation was a continued source of instability in the peninsula. For some years there seemed to be a danger that the Catholic powers of Europe might join in a crusade against Italy to restore the temporal power. In Italy itself an awkward situation was created when the Pope advised his former subjects that it was "not expedient" that they should participate in elections under the new regime. Devout Catholics, heeding the Pope's *non expedit*, withdrew from Italian politics, leaving the field clear for the anti-clericals. The Left came into power in 1876 and established an essentially secular system of public education. Only the advance of Marxian socialism led to the withdrawal of the *non expedit* in 1905. Meanwhile a conflict of loyalties had been created which ultimately weakened both the Church and the state.

The reign of Pius IX was marked by one further Church-State conflict, this time in Germany. Under the leadership of Otto von Bismarck, the largest Protestant state, Prussia, had taken the lead in the process of German unification. Austria was excluded from German affairs after a short war in 1866, and the victory over France brought about the federation of the German states under Prussian leadership in 1871. In the new German empire, from which Catholic Austria had been cut off, the Protestants were in the majority, although there were sizeable Roman Catholic minorities in south Germany, the Rhineland, the Polish districts, and the provinces of Alsace and Lorraine newly conquered from France.

Bismarck was anxious to establish the new empire on firm

foundations, and he was fearful of any element which might endanger the national unity. He saw the Roman Catholic Church, with its international connections, as such a danger. The German Catholics had organized a political party on an essentially confessional basis, the Center party, which Bismarck regarded as anti-national. He was generally fearful of the political behavior of Roman Catholicism with its repeated efforts to obtain action by the powers on behalf of the Pope's temporal sovereignty. Within Germany, he observed that those groups which most resisted German nationalism were Catholic: the provincialists of south Germany, the Poles, the Alsatians. Roman Catholic attempts to repress the Old Catholic schism brought about conflicts with the states, since the professors whom the bishops sought to dismiss were state employees. Finally, Bismarck was politically allied with the anti-clerical National Liberal party. All these factors brought Bismarck into a course of collision with the Roman Catholic Church in Germany.

The struggle, which commenced in 1871, was dubbed by a liberal professor the *Kulturkampf*, the "battle for civilization." In reality, it was a series of state actions which soon degenerated into an outright persecution of Roman Catholicism. In 1871 the Prussian government abolished the Catholic section of the Ministry of Religion, which had hitherto protected the interests of the Church. In 1872 diplomatic relations with the Pope were broken off, and the Jesuits and some other orders were expelled from Germany. The new Minister of Religion, the Liberal Falk, brought forward a systematic program for the control of the Church. By the Falk Laws of May, 1873, the Prussian government demanded control of the education of the clergy and the right of veto over all clerical appointments. The bishops, led by Wilhelm Emmanuel von Ketteler, bishop of Mainz, refused to comply with the new laws. Several bishops and hundreds of priests were imprisoned and others took refuge abroad; most bishoprics and many parishes were deprived of their pastors. The situation was complicated by fears of a French military revival, led by the Catholic monarchists and directed against Germany, and by the resistance of the Polish minority to efforts to Germanize them. In

1875 the financial assistance given by the Prussian state to the Roman Catholic clergy was withdrawn, all religious orders (except those engaged in nursing) were banished, and the religious guarantees of the Prussian constitution were abolished. In some of the other German states, similar measures were directed against the Roman Catholic Church.

All these measures failed of their effect. The overwhelming majority of German Catholics rallied to the support of a Church which took on the aura of martyrdom, and the Center party, ably led by Ludwig Windthorst, grew in strength. Bismarck began to weary of the struggle, which divided rather than united the German empire, expecially after he abandoned his alliance with the Liberals and needed the support of the Center. He found a new enemy to fight—the rising socialist movement. When a new and more diplomatic Pope, Leo XIII, replaced Pio Nono in 1878, an opportunity was opened for a reconciliation between Germany and the Church. Slowly, quietly, the obnoxious measures were allowed to pass into disuse and eventually were repealed. By the 1880's the *Kulturkampf* had come to an end, and the intransigence of Pius IX had been rewarded with a moral victory.

Nonetheless, the reign of Pius IX ended in 1878 in an atmosphere of failure. The dream of a liberal Papacy had long since vanished, and the political objects for which it was sacrificed had themselves been lost. In the political sphere the weaknesses of Pio Nono were most evident; he was no statesman, and he failed to comprehend the nature of the changes that were overtaking the political and social order of Europe. To be sure, his freedom of action was restricted by the doctrines and traditions of the Church, and there was much in secular liberalism with which no religious person could compromise. Yet a more skillful Pope might have found opportunities for moderation and conciliation. The response of Pio Nono was *non possumus:* it is not possible. He committed the Church to an extreme course of intransigence, not only for his lifetime but for several succeeding generations. The integrity of the Roman Catholic faith was preserved, but much else was lost, as the conflict between the Church and the modern world provoked a crisis of conscience for those Catholics who had hoped to reconcile their religious belief with the cultivation of what appeared promising in the political and intellectual developments of the age. As the Church withdrew into a "state of siege," it left the course of European history to be shaped by non-religious forces. The struggle to maintain the union of Church and state resulted in a divorce between the Church and society.

In another sense, however, the Church had always stood in opposition to the world; and in this sense the reign of Pius IX was a period of triumph for the faith. In this era the devotional fruits of the Catholic revival were reaped, and there was a marked and permanent improvement in the religious tone of Catholic life. The organization of the Church was strengthened, and the position of the Papacy at its center reached its highest point. The Pope saw his dogmatic infallibility proclaimed and his governing authority effectively operating, while his person became the object of intense devotion. The modern Papacy, centralized and authoritarian, as it has functioned from the first to the second Vatican Councils, was the work of Pio Nono.

The reign of Pius IX presents most clearly the paradox of nineteenth-century Christianity, the contrast of external failure and internal triumph. In "Catholic" countries, devout Catholics found themselves a minority, increasingly isolated from the dominant trends of society, at the same time as the index of their devotion was steadily rising. In France, for instance, we see in the course of the century the victory of the secular tendencies stemming from the Revolution; in no other country did the influence of the Church over society so markedly decline. Yet France produced more religious orders, more missionaries, more devotional and social movements than any other Catholic nation. The intensification of the faith went hand in hand with its isolation from the larger society. This double process shaped the character of the Roman Catholic Church for nearly a century.

8

Religion in England, 1830–1860

England occupies a place of peculiar importance in modern Church history. The Anglican communion has proven a most lively member of the Christian family. From it, in addition to movements which remained within its bounds, have emerged new branches of Protestantism: the Congregationalists and Baptists in the seventeenth century, and the Methodists in the eighteenth. These English denominations acquired a still greater significance in the nineteenth and twentieth century, for they were the forms of Protestantism most largely exported to the new countries settled by Europeans—the United States and the British colonies—and to the most promising areas of missionary activity among non-Europeans. Great Britain became the greatest industrial and imperial nation of the nineteenth century, and its cultural influence extended throughout the world. The history of the English churches in this period therefore possesses a significance far greater than the number of their members would indicate.

English church history is marked by the paradox of the continuance of a vigorous established Church combined with the extension of effective freedom to its competitors. The "Church of England as by law established" remained the nominal religion of the majority of the population, being especially strong among the upper classes and in rural areas. The "nonconformist" or "dissenting" Protestant denominations claimed about a fifth of the population, largely in the industrial towns, with a much higher percentage of active members and a larger number of congregations than the Anglicans. Until 1828 the established Church maintained a monopoly of public offices, but in that year the Test and Corporation Acts, which had imposed civil disabilities on dissenters, were repealed, and by mid-century all denominations were on an equal legal footing.[1] The Anglican Church, however, retained its emoluments and its connection with the state, and it continued to provide most of the political, intellectual, and religious leadership of the nation.

It is the peculiarity, the glory, and the tribulation of Anglicanism that it is the most comprehensive of Christian denominations. Formed with the deliberate intent of inclusiveness and flexibility, embodying the empiricism of a nation which has never been fond of logical precision, the Church of England has neither committed itself to rigid formulae nor established an efficient discipline, thereby allowing a variety of thought and practice ranging from Calvinism to Catholicism. This unchecked variety has been the source of the fertility and richness of English religious life. At the same time, the lack of definition in Anglicanism seemed to render it unable to make meaningful affirmations, and its establishment as the religious agency of the state made it dependent on secular society to a dangerous degree. In an age of religious decay, such as the early eighteenth century, or of advancing secularism, such as the nineteenth century, what was the value of being the collective religious expression of the nation when the nation was becoming indifferent to religious values?

It was to obviate such a danger by reviving the religious life of the nation that the evangelical movement was commenced. Stressing moral values rather than doctrine, the evangelicals suc-

---

[1] Even after the emancipating acts of 1828 and 1829, non-Anglicans suffered certain disabilities, nearly all of which, however, were later removed. The most notable was the continuance of the monopoly of the great universities, Oxford and Cambridge, in the hands of the Church of England; only in 1871 were dissenters admitted to all academic appointments. The civil disabilities of Jews were relieved in 1858; and atheists were admitted to Parliament after a struggle (the Bradlaugh case) in 1886.

ceeded in infusing the life of nineteenth-century England with a distinctive seriousness and morality which affected many who were not themselves inclined to evangelical religion. "Victorian" has become a byword for a rigidity of conduct and scrupulosity of conscience which lasted long after the original evangelical impulse had spent its force. Success, in fact, was the undoing of the evangelical movement. The later generations of evangelicals did not demonstrate the power and intensity of their forbears; their only great figure after 1830 was the seventh Earl of Shaftesbury, a genuine humanitarian who achieved reforms in the conditions of factory labor. Evangelicalism became fashionable; it was perhaps the largest party within the Church; and it tended to harden into the narrowness of a party, with its own exclusive tenets and special cant. At its worst, evangelicalism could degenerate into smugness or morbidity. Even at its best, evangelicalism was deficient in the realm of theology, in which it offered little more than faith in the sufficiency of the Bible as interpreted by the individual conscience. The doctrine of justification by faith and the experience of conversion came to be interpreted in a more-or-less Calvinistic fashion which repelled many by its harshness. As the moral influence of evangelicalism was diffused throughout the nation, the evangelical movement itself was losing its force.

While evangelicalism had revived the religious life of a segment of the Church of England, many of the abuses of the eighteenth century continued unchecked into the nineteenth. Political influence and landowner patronage placed the more important and better-endowed benefices in the hands of scions of the nobility and gentry. Non-residence and plurality of benefices was common, so that many parishes were not served by their rectors or vicars but by humble curates, usually ill-paid, while rich revenues were enjoyed by clergymen who performed no services. Inequitable distribution of income, non-performance of services, worldly living, and latitudinarian doctrine were combined in many cases with a firm insistence on the privileges and immunities of the Church. This was the "high and dry" Church; and it needed to be reformed.

One impulse for reform came from outside the Church, from

the secular movement of liberalism which, itself indifferent to religion, insisted that all institutions be rationalized so that they might serve their intended purposes. After the passage of the Reform Act of 1832, establishing the predominance of the liberal bourgeoisie in the electorate, a series of reforms were enacted which included the Church within their scope. The first dealt with the Anglican Church of Ireland, which enjoyed a rich and elaborate establishment, although it served only a small fraction of the population. In 1833, ten sees out of twenty-two were abolished, along with those parishes which had no actual church-goers, and the surplus revenues were applied to the poorer clergy. The radical politicians next proposed to readjust the status of the Church of England itself; partly to head this off, and partly to satisfy the evangelical desire for Church reform, in 1835 the government appointed a commission of bishops and laymen, whose reports were later enacted into legislation. By Acts of 1836 and 1837, some dioceses were reorganized, episcopal revenues were more equitably distributed, superfluous church offices were abolished, and the evils of pluralism and non-residence were corrected. The surplus revenues of the Church were to be administered by an Ecclesiastical Commission of bishops and laymen and were used to raise the stipends of the poorer clergy. Another Act of 1836 provided that tithes, hitherto collected in kind and a burden to agriculture, could be commuted for a relatively stable money payment. The result of these acts was a substantial reform of the Church, correcting the most glaring abuses and improving the character and effectiveness of the clergy. By making the Church establishment more useful and less burdensome, these reforms ensured it a new lease on life.

However, the auspices under which the Church had been reformed gave rise to fears that its abolition, rather than its improvement, was the ultimate goal of the reformers. From the time that dissenters and Roman Catholics were admitted to Parliament, it was no longer possible to identify the Church with the state. The Church was now at the mercy of a legislature in which non-Anglicans, and perhaps even infidels, might predominate. Fears of this sort were intensified by the specter of revolution in

1830, by the coming to power in England of the Whig party which catered to radical reformers, and by the growth of the utilitarian philosophy which proposed to submit all institutions to the test of usefulness in promoting the general happiness. The establishment, and perhaps even religion itself, seemed in grave danger. If the Church of England were to survive, it had to rediscover for itself a principle of identity and authority other than the mere fact of establishment by the state.

At the University of Oxford there began a movement of reaction against the religious influence of secular liberalism which was destined to give a new direction to Anglicanism. The leaders of this movement were members of Oriel College, which had earlier produced a school of liberal religious thinkers, the "Noetics," who combined devotion to the Church with sceptical criticism of all doctrines. Now Oriel produced a group of remarkable personalities of a more earnestly religious temperament. Senior among them was John Keble, whose *Christian Year* was one of the most beloved volumes of devotional poetry. Also eminent was Edward Bouverie Pusey, professor of Hebrew. Among the younger leaders were Richard Hurrell Froude, whose early death cut short a fitfully brilliant career, and John Henry Newman, who was destined to become the greatest figure in English religious history in the nineteenth century. The backgrounds of these men were quite varied. The saintly Keble was a brilliant student who had renounced Oxford for the quiet labors of a country parish. Pusey and Froude were of aristocratic families, reared as "High Churchmen" of the old school, yet different in temperament: Pusey the ascetic scholar and Froude the daring intellectual speculator. Newman had been brought up as an evangelical and had passed through a phase of liberalism. They shared the intellectual heritage of the early Anglican divines and a common devotion to the Church.

The immediate cause of the Oxford Movement was the Irish Church Act of 1833, which seemed to presage the spoliation of the Church by the irreligious liberal state. The only basis on which the Church could stand, it now seemed, was to assert an authority of its own, independent of the state. The Oxford

Movement found this in the doctrine that the Church was an institution not of man but of God, part of the one, catholic and apostolic Church professed in the Creed, possessed of a divine commission and authority ordained by Christ and transmitted by the "apostolic succession" of bishops. They emphasized the Catholic element in the Church of England, the role of tradition, sacraments, and authority. This element, they held, was more important than the "Erastian" character of Anglicanism, the fact that its peculiar national form had been established by the act of the state. Instead they asserted the independent authority of the clergy as the successors of the apostles.

The Oxford Movement began with Keble's 1833 sermon on "National Apostasy," in which he argued that the abolition of the Irish bishoprics was an act of sacrilege. The leadership then passed to the younger men, who issued a series of "Tracts for the Times," pamphlets directed to the clergy and the educated classes, which aroused an immense excitement. They were not successful in preventing liberal legislation concerning the Church, but they did create a large party among the clergy, known as "Tractarians" because of the "Tracts for the Times," or as "Puseyites" because Pusey was the best known of their authors, or as "Anglo-Catholics" because of their religious position, or as the "High Church" party because they emphasized the authority of the Church. Newman, who was vicar of the university church of St. Mary's, shaped the thought of a generation of students by his eloquent sermons. There was a definite improvement of the character of the clergy affected by the movement; indeed the tractarians sought personal holiness and the reform of the Church as much as the evangelicals, although they emphasized not the individual conscience guided by the Bible but rather the collective life of the Church in its sacraments and discipline.

To those who were not won over by the "Tracts for the Times" —that is, to a majority of Anglicans—there seemed something strange and suspicious about the Oxford Movement. It appeared vaguely un-English and definitely anti-Protestant. Its sacramentalism, its air of mystery, its emphasis on authority and tradition, and above all its doctrine of a Catholic Church of which the Church of England was but a part, made it appear that the Oxford Movement was coming dangerously close to the position of the Roman Catholic Church and that, in the end, it would lead men to Rome. No sentiment was more universal among Protestant Englishmen than that of "No Popery"; it was a source of distrust which the tractarians could never live down. The evangelicals and the liberals united against them; what was worse, the bishops, whose authority they exalted, showed them no sympathy. In the controversies that ensued, the tractarians had to justify their position in a Church which, by and large, rejected the claims they made on its behalf. In the process, some of them reached a satisfactory intellectual resolution of the problem— and some, after all, went over to Rome.

The first position which Newman, their ablest apologist, asserted was that of the *via media*, the "middle way" which Anglicanism represented between the extremes of Protestantism on the one hand and Romanism on the other. This concept has been central to the subsequent development of the Anglo-Catholic position; but Newman was soon challenged to prove that the *via media* was indeed a viable position in which Anglican thought could rest. In 1841 he published number 90 of the "Tracts for the Times," in which he argued that the Thirty-Nine Articles, the doctrinal formulary of the Church of England, was not incompatible with many Catholic doctrines and practices. He hoped thereby to win some toleration within Anglicanism for his views, but instead he provoked a reaction, and Tract 90 was condemned by the bishops. From this point on, Newman's position in the Church of England became increasingly difficult. He found himself attracted to the Church of Rome, whose catholicity and apostolic descent rested on surer ground than that of England, yet he was repelled by the outward changes in Roman practice from the times of the Church of the Fathers, a period from which he drew his theology. Torn between a deep affection for the Anglican Church and a growing suspicion that the *via media* was untenable, Newman slowly worked out a theory of the development of doctrine to explain the apparent changes in the course of the history of Roman Catholicism. Meanwhile a group of younger men, disciples whom he could not control, such as the rigorously logical William George Ward, were pressing further toward a position almost indistinguishable from that of Rome. When Ward, in a provocative work in 1844, asserted that he felt able to believe the "whole cycle of Roman doctrine" while remaining a clergyman in the Church of England, he was censured by a convocation of the University of Oxford. Newman himself escaped condemnation, but the hostility against his position was manifest.

By 1845 Newman had become convinced that the Church of England was in an essentially false position; that the true and only Catholic Church was that of Rome; and that the objections against Roman doctrine could be resolved by the theory of development, the idea that, while divine revelation is immutable, the Church's conscious formulation of its content develops in the course of its historical growth. In September, 1845, Newman made his submission to the Roman Catholic Church. His example was followed by many of his disciples, and from 1845 there was a steady stream of converts from Anglicanism to the Church of Rome. It was a great accession of strength to that Church in England, and many of the converts took orders and played a large part in the revival of English Catholicism.[2] Newman himself became a priest and wrote many of his most important works —including his autobiographical *Apologia pro vita sua* (1864)— as a Roman Catholic; but he was never fully accepted by his new co-religionists until his last years, when he was made a Cardinal in 1879. The ornament of two Churches, yet never entirely at ease in either, he was too great a man to be the exclusive property of one denomination.

[2] The significance of the Oxford converts was not their number (a few hundred) but their intellectual eminence and ecclesiastical zeal. The numerical growth of Roman Catholicism in England is largely due to massive immigration from Ireland, especially after the famine of 1845. By the end of the century, the Roman Catholics were a significant factor in English religious life, and their continuous growth was greater than that of any major Protestant denomination.

The secession of its most eminent leader and many of its members did not, however, bring about the collapse of the movement which had begun in Oxford. There were those whose loyalty to their ancestral Church remained unaffected and whose distrust of Rome was not overcome by Newman's reasoning. Pusey and Keble were among them, and they rallied together the remainder of their party. The Oxford Movement, however, underwent a change after 1845: it shifted its focus from Oxford to the countryside, to the various parishes served by Oxford graduates and others of Anglo-Catholic views. On this wider, less academic, and more parochial base the movement was able to revive and to survive still further shocks. The most serious of these was the Gorham case in 1850. An evangelical clergyman, Gorham, who denied the doctrine of baptismal regeneration, was refused institution to a parish by his bishop; he appealed to the Privy Council, a largely lay body, which ordered that he be instituted. To the High Churchmen it seemed that the independent authority of the Church had been infringed by the action of the state. There were many who despaired of the Church of England after this decision and went over to Rome; among them was an archdeacon, Henry Edward Manning, the future Cardinal. Yet again Pusey was able to rally the survivors of the movement.

By this time, the high church party should no longer be called the "Oxford Movement" or the "Tractarians." In moving its base from Oxford to the parishes, the party shifted its emphasis from theology to religious practice, especially the element of ritual. "Ritualism," which had never been stressed by the early tractarians, now became the characteristic aspect of the movement as individual parish priests began to revive medieval practices and approximate some of the rites of the Church of Rome. In so doing, they aroused considerable opposition from the evangelicals, who feared all "Romanizing" tendencies, and from many bishops, who found the new rituals contrary to the laws of the Church of England. There were intermittent persecutions as ritualistic priests were prosecuted and occasionally jailed, and the question of ritualism periodically agitated the Church until, in 1896, the failure of a prosecution of a bishop (the Lincoln Judgment) put an end to a conflict which had often verged on the unseemly.

The Anglo-Catholic movement had thus survived, despite numerous crises and extensive secessions. It had, besides establishing itself as a continuing movement within the Church, won some victories. The Convocation of the clergy, suspended since the eighteenth century, was restored in 1852, and the Church at last had an organ of self-expression, though not of self-government. The training of the clergy, hitherto limited to the Bachelor of Arts curriculum, was improved by the erection of theological colleges. Gradually the Anglo-Catholics arrived at a *modus vivendi* with the other elements of the Church.

The Oxford Movement and the evangelicals were not the only parties within the Church of England. There was a third element which regarded both the "High" and "Low" Church as excessively dogmatic and sought to find a way out from their interminable theological disputes by emphasizing other values. This group of liberal Anglicans is often called the "Broad Church" because it valued the inclusiveness of Anglicanism; it stressed the mission of the Church to the nation as a whole. To an extent this represented a continuation of eighteenth-century latitudinarianism. However, it was transformed by elements of evangelical pietism, of Coleridgian mysticism, and of German philosophy and historical research; and it was more affirmatively liberal in theology and more conscious of a social mission. One leader of this group was Thomas Arnold, who—feeling that "the Church, as it now stands, no human power can save"—proposed to throw open Anglican churches to all Christian denominations. As Headmaster of Rugby, Arnold was the founder of the modern British "public school," preaching the ideal of the "Christian gentleman." He shaped the character of many of the leaders of the next generation, among whom was A. P. Stanley, Dean of Westminster, often regarded as the archetypical Broad Churchman.

Another current of Broad Churchmanship centered around Frederick Denison Maurice, the most striking figure in Anglican history after Newman. The son of a Unitarian minister, Maurice entered the Church of England because he saw in it the elements of unity and community which he valued. His own theological views were quite liberal, and when he criticized the conventional doctrine of the eternal death of the reprobate, he was dismissed from his professorship at King's College, London, in 1853. His contemporaries did not realize the depth of his thought, which is more highly regarded in the twentieth century because of its liturgical consciousness and its emphasis on the Church as community.

Maurice was also notable for his association with the short-lived but brilliant Christian Socialist movement, the most striking attempt by Anglicans to respond to the new industrial and social conditions which, though few clergymen realized it, were forcing all religious disputes into the background of modern life. This movement began as a response to the revolution of 1848, which, although it did not spread to England, aroused great fears of social upheaval. J. M. Ludlow, a layman educated in France, called Maurice's attention to the attraction which socialism held for the working classes and the need to Christianize the socialist movement. Maurice and Ludlow were joined by the noted clergyman-novelist, Charles Kingsley, in publishing a series of popular tracts entitled "Politics for the People." They adopted the name Christian Socialists partly to provoke attention but also because they sought a new type of society, essentially non-capitalist, based on the idea of community rather than competition. The practical results of Christian Socialism were the encouragement of cooperative societies and of workers' education. As a movement, Christian Socialism came to an end in 1854, partly because its leaders (except Ludlow) moved on to other concerns. The field of Christian social action had been opened up, but most Churchmen still preferred to confine their efforts in this direction to old-fashioned charity, while the dominant concerns in the Church remained theological. After 1860 liberal views became more influential in the Church, but by then the issues had changed.

The Nonconformist denominations, to whose history we now turn our attention, shared in the intra-religious disputatiousness characteristic of this period, but their interests were more often political than theological. They had, after all, acquired their identity by their refusal to conform to the established Church; and after their political emancipation in 1829 their public activities were directed toward removing the remaining privileges of the Church of England. Despite the fact that they maintained links with the evangelical party among the Anglicans, especially after the founding of the Evangelical Alliance in 1846, many dissenters sought the ultimate abolition of the establishment and advocated the doctrine of voluntaryism. Their strongest spokesman was Edward Miall, leader of the "Liberation Society" and editor of the weekly *Nonconformist,* whose motto was "the dissidence of dissent and the Protestantism of the Protestant religion." It was largely due to Nonconformist objections to governmental support of Anglican schools that England did not establish a public school system until 1870, and then only with safeguards against denominational religious teaching. The "Nonconformist conscience," which played a great role in enforcing the strict public morality that was the heritage of the evangelical revival, expressed itself politically through the Liberal (Whig) party, which was less tied to the established Church than the Conservatives (Tories).

One exception to this usual pattern of Nonconformist political behavior, in the first half of the century, was the Wesleyan Methodist Church, the largest dissenting body. Although they had drawn their early strength from the lower classes, the Wesleyan Methodists retained the political conservatism which they had inherited from Wesley. In addition, they maintained a highly centralized organizational structure, dominated by the Conference of one hundred ministers, whose leader for a long time was Jabez Bunting, often called the "Methodist Pope" because of his dictatorial ways. Discontent with Bunting's political and ecclesiastical conservatism grew, culminating in a crisis in 1847, when a secession took place. Gradually the Wesleyan Methodists liberalized both their church structure and their political habits, and later in the century they joined with other dissenters in the Nonconformist-Liberal alliance.

The dissenters drew their strength largely from the middle class, whose influence was greater in the nineteenth centry than before or since. They shared the virtues and faults of the middle class: sobriety, regularity, "earnestness" (a favorite Victorian catchword), self-sufficiency, narrowness, and a certain drabness in externals. While certain of the older dissenting churches, notably the Quakers and Unitarians,[3] included some extremely wealthy families—the "aristocracy of dissent"—it was more often the case that those who rose higher in the social scale tended to join the establishment. On the other hand, the dissenters (except the Primitive Methodists) were relatively unsuccessful in reaching the lowest end of the scale, the urban proletariat. There was, however, a new outburst of revivalism after 1859, and the Nonconformists were more active in building churches in the new centers of population than were the Anglicans. In Wales, dissent became virtually the national religion. The last third of the century was to be the high point of the vigor and effectiveness of Nonconformity; yet at the same time the foundations of its strength were being sapped by the failure to capture the lowest strata of society.

The outward story of English religion in the Victorian age, as it has been described in these pages, would seem to be one of internal conflict. In a sense, this is a distortion of the reality: the conflicts which occupy so much of the historian's attention took place against a background of widely disseminated faith, a high level of religious activity, and a moral consensus which comprised the substance of the religious life of England. Yet the fact that these conflicts absorbed so much of the attention of the spokesmen of religion is not without significance. The succeeding decades were to witness serious challenges to the churches from

[3] The Unitarians produced one major religious figure, James Martineau, who infused a religious profundity into the rationalism of his denomination.

scientific and intellectual movements and from the rise of the largely unchurched lower classes.[4] The intra-religious conflicts of the period before 1860 left the churches largely unprepared to cope with the external challenges of the latter part of the century.

[4] The religious census of 1851 showed 7,261,032 attendances (3,773,474 Anglican) at Easter services, which represented only 58% of the possible attendance. In the large cities there was accommodation for less than one-third of the population.

9

Protestantism in Northern Europe

In the nineteenth century, the Protestantism of northern Europe exhibited a creativity comparable to that of Britain. Germany, the center of Lutheranism, had the largest body of Protestants on the Continent. Its intellectual influence was even more significant: the philosophical, historical, and theological ideas produced in Germany commanded the attention of the entire learned world. It was the scene of an extensive experiment in church union at the same time as it provoked a striking revival of confessionalism. The confrontation of state churches with evangelical awakenings, and of secular radicalism with Christian social action, made Germany the focus of the practical religious issues of the century. The Scandinavian countries were influenced by many of the same movements, although they produced distinct national variations.

The most significant contribution of nineteenth-century German Protestantism was in the field of theology and religious philosophy. In intellectual matters generally, Germany held a position of leadership throughout the century comparable to that of France in the preceding epoch. German intellectual life was dominated by the universities to an unusual degree, and it is impossible to understand German thought without appreciating its highly academic character. The Reformation itself had begun in the universities, and the theological faculties enjoyed a position of great esteem. From this religious respect for the universities grew the tradition of academic freedom, which allowed a wide latitude of philosophical and religious speculation. Sometimes, indeed, it seemed that speculation could be carried too far: one writer remarked that "to the British belongs the sea, to the French the land, and to the Germans the empire of the air."

In religious thought, the "empire of the air" had been conquered by Schleiermacher and Hegel, and their rival influences remained dominant through the first half of the century. Schleiermacher's disciples, more traditional than their master, took a moderately liberal position in theology. The Hegelians divided sharply into "right" and "left" factions. The former sought to defend Christianity by turning it into metaphysics; the latter, led by the sceptical Ludwig Feuerbach, regarded the Absolute as a mere projection of man himself, and they eventually ceased to be religious.[1] The abstract speculation of Hegelianism was curbed somewhat by the historical school of Tübingen, led by F. C. Baur. Despite his use of Hegelian formulae, Baur's emphasis on the close analysis of documents bore fruit in the solid development of Biblical criticism later in the century. Still another element in the religious thought of the German universities was the so-called "mediating school," influenced by Schleiermacher, which opposed the extremes of pantheistic metaphysics and of rigid orthodoxy. The most eminent representatives of this school were the Church historian Neander, a convert from Judaism, and Richard Rothe, who emphasized the ethical element in Christianity.

Opposed to all these tendencies was the revival of Lutheran orthodoxy, which was given impetus by the resistance to the merger of the Lutheran and Reformed Churches in Prussia after 1817. This revival of confessionalism stressed Church discipline, sacraments, and doctrine. Its outstanding spokesman was an Old Testament scholar at Berlin, E. W. Hengstenberg, who vigorously defended the inspiration of the Scriptures and resisted lib-

[1] The most famous of the "left Hegelians" was Karl Marx, who transformed Hegel's dialectic of the Spirit into "dialectical materialism."

eral tendencies in theology. The ablest group of confessional theologians gathered at Erlangen under the leadership of Adolf von Harless. The Erlangen school, orthodox yet responsive to critical thought, produced the theory of *kenosis* ("self-empty-ing"), which sought to reconcile the humanity of Jesus with the traditional conception of His divinity. The conservative Lu-theran revival, though not of Pietist origin, drew strength from movements of religious awakening among the people. On the other hand, conservative Lutheranism was linked to the court-centered reaction after 1848 by the jurist F. J. Stahl, a convert from Judaism. With its emphasis on authority and church order, the Lutheran revival showed marked affinities with both Roman Catholicism and High Church Anglicanism.

In the latter half of the century the outstanding religious thinker was Albrecht Ritschl, who taught at Göttingen. Trained as an historian, Ritschl sought to expel from theology both the speculative metaphysics of the Hegelians and the subjective indi-vidualism of the Pietists; he wished instead to ground his theol-ogy on the person of Jesus Christ as revealed historically in the Gospels. Contrasting religious with theoretical knowledge, Ritschl argued that faith is based on "value-judgments" [2] by which we know that Christ is God because we find that he has the worth of a God for our souls. The pragmatic cast of Ritschl's mind led him to present Christianity in essentially ethical terms in his great work, *The Christian Doctrine of Justification and Reconciliation* (1870). The two foci of Christianity are redemp-tion, whose object is the Church as the community of believers, and the Kingdom of God, which Ritschl defined as "the organi-zation of humanity through action inspired by love." Through moral action inspired by the example of Christ, Christians work toward the realization of the Kingdom of God.

Ritschl may be regarded as one of the founders of modern liberal Protestantism and a precursor of the "social Gospel." His

[2] The term "value-judgment," which Ritschl coined to express the special character of religious knowledge, has since been appropriated by the social sciences to express the personal element in what Wilhelm Dilthey called the *Geisteswissenschaften* as distinguished from the natural sciences.

work appealed powerfully to the more positive temper of the late nineteenth century, especially in his rejection of Romantic philosophies of religion, his emphasis on the historical reality of Jesus, and his conception of the Church as an ethical community. Essentially optimistic, Ritschl denied the doctrine of original sin and sought the perfection of mankind. His optimism, which has caused his theology to be rejected by the neo-orthodox revival of the twentieth century, made him a source of inspiration to the last generation of the nineteenth.

Ritschl's leading disciples were the theologians Julius Kaftan and Wilhelm Herrmann, who modified his views to some degree, and the church historian Adolf von Harnack. Harnack is notable for his *History of Dogma* (1886–1889), which asserted that primitive Christianity had been transformed and "Hellenized" by its contact with the Graeco-Roman world; the evolution of dogma represented its corruption by the addition of extraneous philosophical elements. Harnack and his generation carried to its furthest point the "quest for the historical Jesus," the attempt through critical scholarship to ascertain the original message of Christianity, which they tended to present in terms of their own liberal theology. Not all liberal theology, however, was Ritschlian. The "history of religions" school, whose most eminent figure was Ernst Troeltsch, criticized Ritschl's exclusive reliance on the Bible and sought to interpret Christianity in more universal and relativistic terms, comparing it with the other religions of the ancient Near East.

Enough has been said, in this brief survey, to indicate the variety and richness of nineteenth-century German religious thought. No one viewpoint ever predominated: Hegel appealed to intellect, Schleiermacher to feeling, Ritschl to ethics, the conservative Lutherans to authority, the biblical critics to the historical documents. It was a many-sided intellectual tournament which fascinated contemporary religious thinkers throughout Europe. Its virtues were those of sincere, scholarly debate; its defect, from a twentieth-century standpoint, was the absence of sense of crisis.

The universities were protected sanctuaries of relative freedom in a Germany which was still dominated by absolutist princes. The Protestant churches reflected in their structure the political situation of Germany, which had been reshaped by Napoleon and the Congress of Vienna into some thirty-nine states. Each state had its own Protestant church (*Landeskirche*) under the ruler as "Supreme Bishop." The principle on which the *Landeskirchen* were based was thus territorial rather than confessional, and the dominance of the rulers left little room for self-government in the churches. Despite a substantial Pietistic awakening, lay participation in the affairs of the Church was not welcomed.

The most striking event in the ecclesiastical history of German Protestantism was the union of the Lutheran and Reformed Churches. The distinctions between these two main streams of Protestantism, separated since the sixteenth century, seemed to have been reduced in significance by the rationalism of the Enlightenment, which minimized the value of dogmas, and by the rising influence of Pietism, with its emphasis on individual religious experience. Fusion was facilitated by the political reshaping of Germany after the Congress of Vienna, which placed many adherents of one confession under a ruler of another faith. In the decade after 1815, unions were achieved in Prussia, Hesse, Nassau, Anhalt, and the Rhenish Palatinate, the areas in which the Reformed elements were most strongly represented. These unions only superficially resembled the ecumenical movement of the twentieth century; rather, they were the products of absolutism and bureaucracy.

The most important union was that which took place in Prussia, the largest German state. King Frederick William III, a second-rate autocrat but a deeply religious man, utilized the tercentenary of the Reformation in 1817 to proclaim the union of the Protestants of his realm. The united church was to be called "Evangelical" rather than Lutheran or Reformed; congregations might hold to the confession of their choice, but communion and church appointments were open to all. Although the strict Lutheran Claus Harms published ninety-five theses denouncing the union and calling for the maintenance of confessional standards, the union was generally well received until, in 1822, the king decreed a common liturgy, the *Agenda*, for all churches. His minister Altenstein had convinced him that he could act autocratically by virtue of his prerogative as Supreme Bishop; but protests arose against the new liturgy and the royal interference in religious affairs. Schleiermacher joined in the protests, and eventually variant forms of liturgy were permitted. In the course of time a complex ecclesiastical organization of synods, consistories, and superintendents was created for the Evangelical Church of Prussia.

The protests against the union which had commenced with Harms' theses grew into a substantial revival of conservative confessional Lutheranism. States in which the Reformed were not strongly represented, such as Saxony, Mecklenburg, Hanover, and some parts of Bavaria, maintained strictly Lutheran Churches. Within Prussia there were areas of resistance, notably in Silesia, where a congregation sought to secede from the state church. The "Old Lutheran" dissenters were persecuted until the death of Frederick William III in 1840; his successor allowed them to organize an independent church. The strict Lutherans were dominant in the German migration to the United States where several Midwestern synods, notably the Missouri Synod founded by K. F. W. Walther, perpetuate their influence. The center of confessional Lutheranism was the Protestant section of northern Bavaria, where the theological faculty of Erlangen was located. The greatest figure in the movement was Wilhelm Löhe, pastor of Neuendettelsau, which he transformed into a center of practical Christian activity. In addition to his social work and his support of the Lutheran emigration to America, Löhe is significant as the founder of the Lutheran liturgical movement; his emphasis on the sacraments and private confession and his high doctrine of the Church have contributed much to the outlook and practices of conservative Lutheranism.

Despite the revival of Lutheran orthodoxy, it was not the confessional principle but the territorial Church which dominated the German scene; and the Evangelical Church of Prussia was the largest Protestant body on the continent. Schleiermacher had called it a "Court Church" to emphasize its dependence on royal authority, and it was throughout the century an organ of political conservatism of an aristocratic or patriarchal character, emphasizing obedience to the state and acceptance of the social order. Under the romantic and somewhat unstable Frederick William IV in the 1840's there were a number of tentative experiments both with bishops and with synods; but a general synod which met in 1846 accomplished no results. The revolution of 1848 seemed to promise more freedom for the church, and an all-German *Kirchentag* was held which became an annual meeting; but the reaction after 1848 turned state and church back to more conservative courses. After 1860 greater scope was allowed for congregational councils and district and provincial synods, but the ultimate authority of the crown was maintained. Bismarck, the architect of German unification in 1870, symbolized the adjustment too easily made by German Protestants: deeply religious in his personal life, he nonetheless felt that the state must pursue its course without regard to moral scruples, and his religious sense of duty only strengthened his commitment to a state based on naked power. As Marxism grew in strength among the working classes, the role of the church in the defense of the social order was emphasized, and the German emperors patronized a religious system which they regarded as a bulwark of their power.

The one outlet for voluntary initiative in the German churches was in the field of philanthropic social activity—the Inner Mission, as it came to be called, which represented the practical effort of Christians to meet the needs of the poor and displaced in the changing conditions of modern society. Systematic effort, as distinguished from occasional charity, may be said to have begun with the work of Theodor Fliedner, pastor at Kaiserswerth, who built up a set of institutions in his parish, including a hospital, staffed by women called "deaconesses" who devoted themselves to the care of the poor. Kaiserswerth became a center for the training of deaconesses and, along with the similar center founded by Amalie Sieveking in Hamburg, served to inspire the work of Florence Nightingale and the development of professional nursing. At Neuendettelsau Löhe developed a similar set of institutions, although the conservative Lutherans tended generally to be suspicious of lay activity.

The great organizer of the Inner Mission was J. H. Wichern, a pastor in Hamburg, where he recognized the alienation of the growing mass of workers from churches which were directed to the middle and upper classes. Especially concerned for the children of the urban poor, Wichern opened a home for destitute boys, the "Rough House," in 1833. The Rough House became the center of a set of institutions of social work served by an order of men called deacons. Wichern, a born organizer, saw the Inner Mission as the beginning of a true people's church (*Volkskirche*) in which works of love would unite all classes in a Christian community. At the *Kirchentag* of 1848 Wichern's preaching brought about the organization of a national Central Committee for the Inner Mission, which met at the annual *Kirchentagen*. Wichern's work was patronized by the Prussian royal house. With all his recognition of the clash of social classes and his vision of a people's church, Wichern was a social and political conservative; he regarded the Inner Mission as an antidote to materialistic socialism and a bulwark of the existing social order. The *Volkskirche* was identified with the actual *Landeskirchen;* and the Inner Mission became in time merely a series of organized charities under the patronage of the established church and state.

The *Volkskirche* came closer to realization in solidly Lutheran Scandinavia than in religiously divided Germany. In each of the northern countries the church, tied to the state as in Germany, was a symbol of the national identity. While the intellectual contribution of the Scandinavian churches was less significant than that of Germany, they experienced awakenings and revivals with a more extensive basis of popular support. In the classic pattern of Protestant Europe, the revivals had to contend, at the beginning of the century, with an entrenched rationalism in church and state and, as democracy advanced during the latter part of the period, with growing religious indifference among the masses.

In Denmark the revival, which was associated with a general renascence of Danish cultural life, was dominated by the figure of Nicolai Grundtvig. After an experience of conversion, Grundtvig developed a strong consciousness of the role of the church as a living community in which Christ acts in the sacraments of baptism and communion. Grundtvig's work at once strengthened the established church and gave it a more popular base. He shared in the revival of national culture, reviving the study of Nordic mythology and writing histories and hymns; his development of "folk schools" made him the forerunner of modern adult education and contributed to the growth of an educated Danish national consciousness. Grundtvigianism was an unusual combination of patriotism with religious revival. Other leaders of the Danish revival, such as Bishop Mynster and the theologian Martensen, differed from Grundtvig in their emphases; and critical of them all was the lonely figure of Kierkegaard, whose radical doctrines were not appreciated until the twentieth century.

The revival in Norway was closely related to the struggle for national identity against the influences first of Denmark and, after 1814, of Sweden, from which Norway did not obtain full independence until 1905.[3] The Norwegian revival was associated, more than in Denmark or Sweden, with Pietism. It was begun at the turn of the century by Hans Nielsen Hauge, a layman, who appealed to the independent farmer class which was characteristic of Norway. Hauge commenced a movement of lay preachers or "readers" which, despite the restrictions of the laws against conventicles, continued even after Hauge himself was silenced. The Haugean revival, although a movement of laymen often critical of the clergy, remained within the state church; and later revivals stimulated the clergy as well as the laity. The pattern of revival in Norway was one of groups of pious laymen,

---

3 In this regard the Norwegian revival was similar to that of Finland, which was an autonomous portion of the Russian empire, often threatened with the loss of its national identity. The Lutheran Church of Finland served as an expression of national unity. It was strongly affected by Pietism.

often with their own "prayer houses," working within the framework of the national Church.

The story of Sweden is more complex. On the one hand there were extensive lay revivals under Pietistic influences; on the other hand there was a growing high church movement which emphasized the role of the ordained clergy.[4] More than in the other Scandinavian countries the popular revivals led to substantial secessions from the established church; of these sects, the most notable was the Swedish Mission Covenant led by Karl Olof Rosenius. As in the other northern countries, toleration was eventually extended to dissident groups, but Sweden went further in the direction of allowing self-government within the established church. Sweden, the most industrialized of the Scandinavian states, illustrated most clearly the limitations of the nineteenth-century revivals: the materialistic Social Democratic movement grew rapidly in strength, moral standards seemed to be lowered, and only a minority—albeit an active minority—was deeply committed to religion.

The most difficult problem in evaluating the significance of the revivals and intellectual contributions of northern European Protestantism is assessing the extent to which these developments affected the mass of the population. This problem is complicated by the growth of an urban proletariat, a new class which presented challenges to churches which had been organized in a patriarchal agrarian society, and by the curious fact that the extensive emigration, particularly to America, was more powerfully affected by the new religious movements than was the population which remained in the home countries. On the one hand it may be said that the recurrent revivals indicated the latent strength of traditional belief and religious behavior (baptism and confirmation were almost universal) and the extent to which Pietism had pervasively influenced the life of the nation. On the other hand, the revivals reached only a minority of the population; and the intellectual movements, with their strongly aca-

---

[4] The Swedish Church resembled the Anglican in that it maintained the tradition of apostolic succession of bishops.

demic flavor, were even more limited in their appeal. It is perhaps significant that the official Churches did little to encourage most of the new movements, which drew their strength from independent initiative, often of laymen, and which never succeeded in transforming an entire church. As in Roman Catholic countries, the intimate connection of the church with the state and with the existing social order was the decisive fact which limited the effect of any revival. Yet in its proliferation of new currents of thought, however restricted in their immediate consequences, nineteenth-century European Protestantism demonstrated a creativity whose effects are still being felt.

10

The Reformed Churches

The history of the Reformed Churches in the nineteenth century presents a recurrent pattern of church-state conflicts. Movements of awakening in the churches, combining evangelicalism with a revival of Calvinist orthodoxy, came into conflict with a rationalistic church leadership supported by the secularizing power of the liberal state.[1] The result was a series of secessions or "disruptions," in which the stricter and sterner party withdrew from the established churches and sought, by means of voluntary separation, to obtain that perfected church polity which their ancestors had pursued with the aid of the coercive power of the state. These conflicts, unlike those in Germany and England, contributed little to the development of theology, but they added new dimensions to the concept of religious liberty.

In Scotland, the Kirk—the Presbyterian established Church—held a position of distinctive importance in the life of the nation. Since the political union with England in 1707, the Kirk had been the popular symbol of Scottish national identity. The eighteenth century had seen some sapping of harsh Calvinistic doc-

[1] An exception to this pattern was the large Reformed Church in Hungary, which was confronted with the Roman Catholic government of the Austrian Empire. Toleration had been conceded by Joseph II, but full legal equality was definitively obtained only in 1867. The Hungarian Calvinists produced no outstanding religious leaders or movements comparable to those of the West.

trine by rationalism, but in general the clergy maintained a strict orthodoxy.[2] Rather, as is often the case in Calvinistic churches, issues of church discipline provided the sources of conflict. The Scottish Kirk possessed an organ of self-government, the General Assembly, but it was nonetheless subject to the state—that is, to a Parliament dominated by Englishmen. Lay patronage, the right of landowners to nominate ministers, was a source of irritation and a symbol of the denial of liberty to the Church. Patronage was supported by the Moderate party, somewhat worldly and rationalistic, and opposed by the Evangelical party, which combined rigid orthodoxy with a desire for reform.

The leader of the Evangelicals was Thomas Chalmers, who sought to bring the Christian ministry to the lower classes, especially in the towns. The Evangelical party grew in strength among the clergy and began a ten years' struggle in 1833 to bring about the abolition of patronage, the great hindrance to reform. In 1834 the General Assembly passed an Act giving the parishioners the right to reject the patron's nominee, but the House of Lords, judging a test case in 1839, decided in favor of the rights of the patrons. A protest by the Assembly in 1842 went unheeded by Parliament. In 1843 Chalmers led a dramatic secession of one-third of the ministers, who sacrificed their appointments and security to assert the independence of the Church. They were followed by over one-third of the laity and all the foreign missionaries, who joined them in founding the Free Church of Scotland.

The "disruption," as it was called, did not mean an acceptance of the principle of voluntaryism: "We quit a vitiated Establishment," said Chalmers, "but would rejoice in returning to a pure one." The Free Church, starting without buildings or endowment, experienced an outburst of enthusiasm which resulted in the building of five hundred churches in ten years and the rapid

2 Calvinistic orthodoxy drove from the Kirk an unusual minister, Edward Irving, who was expelled in 1833 for his support of faith-healing and speaking with tongues. He preached apocalyptic and prophetic doctrines and founded the Catholic Apostolic Church (Irvingites), which was remarkable for its liturgical innovations.

collection of funds to establish the organization on a solid footing. The disruption took from the established Church its best
leaders, but it was followed by a revival of church life in both the
new and the old bodies. The grievance which had prompted the
disruption was removed by the abolition of patronage in 1874,
but the Scottish churches were not reunited until 1929.[3]

Switzerland, the homeland of Reformed Protestantism, experienced the pattern of rationalism, revival, and disruption that
characterized nineteenth-century Calvinism. The Swiss situation
was made complex by the fact that each of the cantons had its
own established church. In 1848 the liberal party, victorious in
the recent war of the *Sonderbund,* established a new constitution
which provided for freedom of religion and residence throughout
the Confederation, and the voluntary nature of religious affilia-
tion was further guaranteed in 1874. However, while the liberals
secured the rights of the individual believer, they were prone to
interfere with the freedom of the churches as corporate religious
bodies. In several cantons, conflicts broke out on the issue of the
freedom of the church from state control.

A revival (the *réveil*) began in Geneva after 1810, partly under
Moravian influences and partly due to the work of a visiting
Scottish evangelical, Robert Haldane. Among those influenced
by Haldane was a minister, César Malan, who became a noted
hymn-writer. Haldane and Malan were opposed by the official
organization of the Genevan clergy, the Venerable Company of
Pastors, which had succumbed to the rationalism of the eight-
eenth century and had effectively abandoned dogmatic belief.
The Venerable Company forbade preaching on the divinity of
Christ, sin, grace, or predestination; eventually Malan was forced
out of the church. He formed an independent congregation in
Geneva and travelled extensively elsewhere. In 1831 an evangeli-

[3] There had been previous secessions from the Kirk in the eighteenth
century, largely on the issue of resistance to State control. In 1900 the church
which had resulted from these secessions merged with the Free Church. A
small minority of the Free Church—the "Wee Frees"—rejected the merger,
claimed to be the true Free Church and won a lawsuit to obtain its property.
The matter was finally adjusted by an act of Parliament.

cal society was formed in Geneva, which founded its own theological seminary the next year; in 1849 the Free Church of Geneva was organized. Slowly, through the century, the evangelicals penetrated even within the ranks of the Venerable Company itself; and by the time the Church of Geneva was disestablished, early in the twentieth century, a majority of its ministers were evangelicals.

The struggle was more intense in the canton of Vaud, where the liberal civil authorities sought to establish full state control over the church. Evangelical conventicles, formed under the influence of the *réveil*, were met with persecution in the 1820's. In 1839 the government abolished the Helvetic Confession, the dogmatic symbol of the Church, and the structure of church government above the parish level. In 1845 a majority of the ministers and many of the theological faculty at Lausanne resigned, organizing the Free Church of Vaud in 1847. The movement was one primarily of the clergy and did not receive popular support. It was notable, however, because it produced one of the greatest spokesmen on freedom of conscience, Alexandre Vinet. Vinet protested against the actions of the civil authorities and withdrew from the official church. He advocated voluntary church membership and the separation of church and state on the ground of the supremacy of conscience.

One other secession church emerged from the struggle of the evangelicals with the state churches. In 1873 half the congregations of Neuchatel, aroused by government curtailment of the freedom of the Synod, seceded and formed an Independent Evangelical Church. In the German-speaking cantons the conflict, though severe, did not result in secessions. Here the issue was more clearly theological: the evangelicals defended the orthodox faith against opponents who imported liberal doctrines from the German universities. The parties were evenly matched, and the result was a wide variation in doctrine and practice. The liberals eventually abandoned the effort to use the power of the state to control the churches, but the victory of the evangelicals was far from complete. However, their work had repercussions in other countries, notably France.

The political situation of the Reformed Church in France was quite different from that in Switzerland. The Huguenots, less than two per cent of the population, had only emerged from persecution at the time of the Revolution. In 1802, as part of his ecclesiastical settlement, Napoleon enacted organic laws for the Reformed Church in France, which thus received official recognition. Pastors were to be supported by the state, which exercised rigid supervision over the church, depriving it of most of its autonomy; the affairs of the church were entrusted to a government-appointed general board, and congregational organization was restricted. The Huguenots, still under the influence of the ideas of the Enlightenment, accepted this arrangement without protest. It was continued under the governments of the Restoration, although the Protestants were occasionally subjected to harassment. The French Protestants rose to a position of disproportionate influence in the intellectual, economic, and political life of the nation; one of them, Guizot, was Prime Minister under Louis Philippe.

Under the influence of British evangelicals and the Genevan *réveil*, an evangelical awakening began in France after 1817. Missionaries traveled widely, notably the ex-soldier Felix Neff, who preached in the Alpine valleys and revived the faith of the Waldensians, a Protestant sect older than the Reformation. In 1818 a Bible Society was formed, followed by a religious tract society in 1821 and an organization for foreign missions in 1822. The brothers Frédéric and Adolphe Monod, educated in Geneva, began a revival of Calvinistic orthodoxy. By 1848, the French Reformed Church, like those of Switzerland, was divided into evangelical and rationalistic parties. The revolution of that year afforded the opportunity to hold a national synod which, however, was unable to reach agreement on matters of doctrine. The failure to adopt a confession of faith provoked Frédéric Monod to lead a secession which resulted in the formation of a free church, unsupported by the state. In 1852, Napoleon III modified the constitution of the state-supported Reformed Church, reconstituting the elected congregational and regional organizations. In the succeeding decades the differences between evangelicals and liberals deepened, and when, after the fall of Napoleon, the church was free to hold national synods, the annual meetings became battlegrounds between the two parties. The liberals found themselves in a minority, and the Synod of 1872 drew up an orthodox confession of faith, to which, however, many were unwilling to subscribe. The sharply-divided parties remained tenuously bound together in a common church, which succeeded, despite these quarrels, in expanding its activities, particularly in the cities. When, in 1905, the separation of church and state was enacted, the Reformed of France divided into three distinct churches, representing orthodox, liberal, and moderate factions.

In Holland the internal conflict of the Reformed Church produced its most interesting variations. After a period of turmoil during the wars of the French Revolution, the Dutch Church was given a new constitution by the first king of the Netherlands, William I, in 1816. William's *Reglement* in effect abolished the autonomy of the Church, placing it under a general synod appointed by the state and subordinated to the Ministry of Worship. Only after 1852 was the freedom of the Church partially restored. Rationalistic influences predominated among the clergy, who were not strictly bound to orthodoxy.

An evangelical revival began in the early 1820's, partly under the influence of romanticism and partly stimulated by the Genevan *réveil*. The revival, unlike those in other Reformed churches, was led largely by laymen, of whom the most striking was Isaak da Costa, a converted Jew. Another leader was Groen van Prinsterer, who organized a political party, the Anti-Revolutionary party, to defend the interests of the church, particularly in education. The Dutch revival stressed Calvinist orthodoxy and received considerable support from the common people, among whom traditional beliefs had not been weakened by the Enlightenment. Out of the cleavage between the congregations and the official Church came a secession in 1834. This resulted in the formation of the Christian Reformed Church, a free church about one-tenth the size of the parent body, which played a large part in the Dutch migration to America.

In the second half of the century the situation became more favorable for the orthodox revival. Political change brought about greater freedom for religious movements and an eventual expansion of the franchise. The Anti-Revolutionary party was strengthened by the larger franchise and the leadership supplied by an able pastor and politician, Abraham Kuyper. Education was the chief political issue. The state-supported schools, organized by liberal governments, were religiously neutral, and orthodox Calvinists sought to organize private schools on a confessional basis. Kuyper was able to win a state subsidy for the religious schools in 1887 by forming an expedient alliance with the Roman Catholics, who had also organized a school system; and from 1901 to 1905 he was prime minister at the head of a coalition ministry. Meanwhile, in 1880, he had led in the formation of the Free University of Amsterdam, intended to combat the rationalism which still prevailed in the state universities. From the movement led by Kuyper emerged a new secession from the state Church in 1886, which merged with the Christian Reformed Church in 1892.

The established Church, which still claimed a majority of the population, was thus confronted at the end of the century by a formidable rival. The unique feature of the secession church of the Netherlands, which differentiated it from the secessions in other Reformed bodies, was that it was paralleled by a political organization and an educational establishment of considerable importance. A movement which had begun as an effort to Christianize the state produced instead a separate church. The case of the Netherlands illustrates how the revival in the Reformed churches, combining evangelicalism with Calvinist orthodoxy, resulted in a heightening of the confessional consciousness.

11

Science and Conscience

If the first half of the nineteenth century was a period of religious revival, the second half must be regarded as a period of religious crisis. The limitations of the revival became evident when it was confronted by the dominant secular tendencies of the age. From the 1860's, the churches were faced with external challenges: in the intellectual sphere, from natural science and biblical criticism; in the area of social policy, from the advance of democracy and the needs of the industrial masses. We must examine each of these challenges in turn.

The intellectual challenges, focused around the year 1860, have a deceptive appearance of suddenness. It should be remembered that the nineteenth century—the "age of ideology"—was prolific of intellectual movements, not all of which can be neatly categorized. Side by side with Romanticism, which had given strength to the revival of religion, were movements which drew from the heritage of the Enlightenment: the utilitarianism of Bentham and the Mills, or the "positive philosophy" of Auguste Comte.[1] After mid-century, the Romantic outlook tended to be

[1] Comte's positivism, with its theory of the progress of mankind through stages to an age of "positive" science and social organization, was essentially rationalistic. However, Comte sought to obtain for his ideals the power and attractiveness of a religion. His "Religion of Humanity" was organized with all the trappings of a church. It has been called "Catholicism minus Christianity." Positivism is an extreme example of the tendency of non-religious social movements to function as secular or substitute religions.

125

supplanted by a harsher "realism," which sought not to transcend but to face the reality of modern life—preferably its more
disagreeable aspects. These movements largely drew their
strength from those who had not been affected by the revival of
religion. What was distinctive about the crises of the 1860's was
that they challenged most directly those whose training and motives were basically religious.

The nineteenth-century crisis of conscience, like that of the
late seventeenth century, occurred when beliefs regarded as essential to orthodox religion were confronted by modern discov-
eries supported by verifiable evidence. An American historian,
Andrew D. White, has called this "the warfare of science with
theology." This, however, is to miss the point of the conflicts over
evolutionary biology and biblical criticism: it was not the scientific challenge, but the religious response, that was crucial. In
these conflicts, the spokesmen of the churches chose to narrow the
ground on which Christianity was to be defended, and they allowed their opponents to appear more reasonable and honest
than themselves. In the conflicts of the 1860's, the position of
morality was the position opposed to orthodox doctrine. We may
call this "the warfare of conscience with theology."

Even before the churches felt the impact of the scientific challenge, sensitivity of conscience was a productive source of discontent. In Roman Catholic countries the discontent was usually of
a political nature: Lamennais is the most striking example of
those who could not reconcile their sense of justice with the
reactionary politics of the Church. The case of Döllinger, however, indicates that intellectual conflicts might alienate from
Roman Catholicism those who had been its staunchest defenders.
It is, however, among Protestants, and particularly in the English-
speaking world, that the alienation of the intellectuals from religion took most clearly the form of a moral crisis. The self-exami-
nation of conscience engendered by evangelicalism produced a
sub-surface current of doubt along with the rising tide of faith.
In some cases, the source of doubt was the discrepancy between
the essentially other-worldly concern of the evangelicals and the
aspirations of the age toward the progress and improvement of

human society. In other cases, the source of doubt was an ethical revulsion against the sterner Christian doctrines—reprobation, eternal punishment, vicarious atonement—which appeared to sensitive souls to be cruel, capricious, and even immoral, "attributing to God," as Darwin said, "the feelings of a revengeful tyrant." Perhaps evangelicalism had made men too moral and humanitarian to be strictly orthodox. Even before the impact of evolutionary science and biblical criticism, Christian dogma was being undermined by objections on ethical grounds.

The most direct challenge to conventional orthodoxy came from the scientific concept of development or evolution, the idea that the world of nature was not suddenly created in its present form but rather developed from simpler forms over long periods of time by the regular action of scientific laws. The idea of evolution, which paralleled the historicism so congenial to the age, challenged not only the traditional religious doctrine of creation but also the static outlook of eighteenth-century science. The first great advance of evolutionary science was in the field of geology, in which observers had noticed the superimposition of strata and the occurrence of fossils of species no longer in existence. Sir Charles Lyell's *Principles of Geology* (1830–1833) convincingly propounded the uniformitarian hypothesis that geological formations were the products not of sudden catastrophes but of the slow operation of processes of change. This viewpoint required a longer time-span of geological history than seemed to be allowed by the biblical account of creation. Some theologians were able to resolve the difficulty by reinterpreting the "days" of *Genesis* as geological epochs. Fossils, however, were more difficult to account for, and one religiously-minded scientist was driven to the ingenious hypothesis that they had been deliberately placed by God in order to test man's faith.

When the developmental approach was extended from geology to biology, more serious problems arose. Evolutionary theories had been suggested in the eighteenth century and were revived in more definite form by Lamarck in the 1820's; but such views were rejected by most biologists, who were then more interested in classifying than in explaining the variation of species. The idea of evolution, however, was "in the air." An amateur, Robert Chambers, published anonymously in 1844 his *Vestiges of the Natural History of Creation,* which asserted that each species had not been specially created by God but had evolved in accordance with general laws. This rather unscientific work, written in a spirit of reverence, was greeted by a storm of theological criticism which foreshadowed the more serious debate provoked by Darwin.

The storm over the *Vestiges* was a symptom of the unsettlement of men's minds produced by the scientific picture of impersonal Nature functioning without divine interposition, a picture difficult to resist, yet more difficult to accept:

> Are God and Nature then at strife,
>   That Nature lends such evil dreams?
>   So careful of the type she seems,
> So careless of the single life,
>
> That I, considering everywhere
>   Her secret meaning in her deeds,
>   And finding that of fifty seeds
> She often brings but one to bear,
>
> I falter where I firmly trod,
>   And falling with my weight of cares
>   Upon the world's great altar-stairs
> That slope through darkness up to God,
>
> I stretch lame hands of faith, and grope,
>   And gather dust and chaff, and call
>   To what I feel is Lord of all,
> And faintly trust the larger hope.

So wrote the poet-laureate Tennyson

> Who trusted God was love indeed,
>   And love Creation's final law—
>   Though Nature, red in tooth and claw
> With ravine, shrieked against his creed—

in 1850, almost a decade before the *Origin of Species.* Tennyson's *In Memoriam* is the perfect example of the Victorian mind at equipoise, unable to resist the progress of science, yet hopefully affirming its faith in "the truths that never can be proved."

The intellectual world was thus half prepared for evolutionary biology when Charles Darwin published his *Origin of Species* in 1859. What made Darwin's book the definitive and successful exposition of the theory of evolution was, first, its clear, careful and detailed presentation of massive evidence and, secondly, the fact that Darwin offered a satisfactory theory of the mechanism of evolution, the theory of natural selection. In the struggle for existence, those individuals who possess variations best fitted for their environment will survive and propagate their variations; by the selection of favorable variations over many generations, new species will be evolved. Although Darwin at first refrained from applying this theory to the descent of man, its applicability was immediately recognized. While there might be scientific objections to many aspects of Darwin's theory,[2] the storm that arose over his book focused on his denial of the special creation of each species by direct Divine action and his implicit refusal to assign to man a special place apart from the rest of the biological world. Philosophically it was still more subversive: Darwin's concept of random variations challenged not merely biblical literalism, but also the Deistic argument from design.

The heated debate which followed the publication of the *Origin of Species* took the unfortunate form of a direct confrontation of science and religion.[3] In England, and later in America, the great majority of the spokesmen of religion condemned

[2] Not all scientists accepted Darwinian evolution, and many of his religious opponents were able to shelter themselves behind the views of eminent biologists such as Sir Richard Owen. These scientists, however, were themselves often motivated by religious or philosophical prejudgments rather than by purely scientific reasoning. The most serious scientific objection to Darwin's theory was his inability to explain how variations occurred. This difficulty was only removed after 1900 with the recognition of genetic mutations.

[3] The popular notion of the debate was best expressed by the politician Disraeli: "The question is this—Is man an ape or an angel? . . . I am on the side of the angels."

the theory of evolution, without regard to its scientific merits, on the ground of its repugnance to the text of the Bible and its tendency to degrade man to the level of the beasts. On the other hand, the majority of scientists accepted evolution as a probable hypothesis. In the face of clerical opposition, the spokesmen of Darwinism—notably T. H. Huxley in England and Ernst Haeckel in Germany—took an increasingly anti-religious position. Both sides tended to identify the substance of Christianity with the literal text of *Genesis,* thus making the conflict sharper —and more absurd—than it ought to have been.

The most striking confrontation of the two points of view took place at Oxford in 1860. The Bishop of Oxford, Samuel Wilberforce,[4] acting as the champion of orthodoxy, chose to refute Darwinism by sarcasm, asking Huxley "Was it through his grandfather or his grandmother that he claimed his descent from a monkey?" Huxley's reply was simple but crushing: "He was not ashamed to have a monkey for his ancestor; but he would be ashamed to be connected with a man who used great gifts to obscure the truth." By his emphasis on the supreme virtue of truth-telling, Huxley had turned Victorian morality against Victorian orthodoxy. Wilberforce was discredited, and the intellectual respectability of orthodox religion was imperiled.

Among the rising generation of intellectuals, the victory of evolution was virtually complete. By the end of the century, the majority even of theologians had ceased to oppose the doctrine,[5] turning their endeavors to the assertion of the spiritual uniqueness of man. In this regard, however, the challenge of natural science was reinforced by social science. The anthropological study of primitive societies proved disconcerting to those who

[4] Samuel Wilberforce, the son of the great evangelical leader, was himself a High Churchman, with a distinguished record as a bishop. His popularity-seeking won him the nickname "Soapy Sam."

[5] This statement should be limited to the case of European Protestantism. In America the debate had to be re-enacted a half-century later, in the controversy over "fundamentalism." The Roman Catholic reaction (at first less hostile than the Protestant) is a special case, largely determined by the reaction to biblical criticism in its later "modernist" form.

upheld the universality of the moral code. The idea of evolution was applied to man in a form which emphasized the struggle for existence, rather than love, as the basis of society. The leader of the "social Darwinists" was the philosopher Herbert Spencer, who had coined the phrase "survival of the fittest" and whose picture of society was one of individualistic competition with no pity for those who, having failed, were clearly unfitted for survival. Even Huxley had to protest against the misappropriation of biological evolution as a substitute for social ethics, urging that "intelligence and will . . . may modify the conditions of existence." But the general tendency of post-Darwinian thought was heavily naturalistic or materialistic.

The result of these developments was the alienation of the majority of the intellectual elements from organized religion. Many became outright atheists, having no need of religion to explain a universe which they saw in purely natural terms. Others adopted the position for which Huxley invented the name "agnostic," holding

> that a deep sense of religion was compatible with the entire absence of theology. Secondly, science and her methods gave me a resting-place independent of authority and tradition. . . . Science seems to me to teach in the highest and strongest manner the great truth which is embodied in the Christian conception of entire surrender to the will of God. Sit down before the fact as a little child, be prepared to give up every preconceived notion, follow humbly wherever and to whatever abysses nature leads, or you shall learn nothing.

Truthfulness had replaced belief as the moral standard; but significantly the abandonment of belief did not necessarily represent an abandonment of morality. For those who sought a substitute for Christianity, the "religion of humanity" held a powerful attraction. In the writings of George Eliot (Mary Ann Evans), evangelical morality—the creed of duty, service, and love—stands alone and triumphant, unaided by belief in God or the hope of personal immortality:

> O may I join the choir invisible
> Of those immortal dead who live again

In minds made better by their presence; live
In pulses stirred to generosity,
In deeds of daring rectitude, in scorn
For miserable aims that end with self,
In thoughts sublime that pierce the night like stars,
And with their mild persistence urge man's search
To vaster issues.
              So to live is heaven:
To make undying music in the world,
Breathing as beauteous order that controls
With growing sway the growing life of man.
                    . . .
    May I reach
That purest heaven, be to other souls
The cup of strength in some great agony,
Enkindle generous ardor, feed pure love,
Beget the smiles that have no cruelty—
Be the sweet presence of a good diffused,
And in diffusion ever more intense.
So shall I join the choir invisible
Whose music is the gladness of the world.

In its purest aspirations, the morality of the unbelievers could challenge the best that Christianity had to offer. The search for truth in science is an activity as religious in spirit, if not in form or object, as the search for truth in religion. Thus we may speak of the "religion of unbelief"—the faith of those who found the prevailing orthodoxy incompatible with the scientific truths of which they were convinced, and who chose to follow the truth they saw wherever it might lead. Both their confidence in science and their hostility to religion were in large part misplaced; but their errors were due as much to the blunders of their orthodox adversaries as to their own aggressiveness.

The challenge presented by evolutionary science, serious though it was, was superficial compared with the challenge presented by biblical criticism. The former dealt primarily with the creation account in *Genesis* while the latter ranged over the entire text and interpretation of the Bible. Further, while biblical criticism received less popular attention than the scientific debate, it touched more deeply the sources of the Christian faith. It was an internal rather than an external challenge. Especially among Protestants, for whom the Bible was the ultimate religious authority, the scholarly re-examination of the basic documents of Christianity was a matter of profound interest and concern.

Biblical criticism is the study of the Bible employing the scholarly techniques of literary and historical analysis. Such a study was inevitable in an age which was attracted to the historical approach and in which history itself was becoming increasingly "scientific" and objective in its methodology. One application of this approach was the so-called "lower criticism," the attempt to establish the correct text of the books of the Bible. This effort proceeded continuously throughout the century, marked by such accomplishments as Tischendorf's discovery of the *Codex Sinaiticus* and Westcott and Hort's edition of the New Testament. Such work was often undertaken in a spirit of reverence, and it was never as controversial as the "higher criticism," the examination of the authorship, sources, motivation, and accuracy of the biblical documents. The results of such examination could easily be disconcerting to those who believe in the direct and literal Divine inspiration of the biblical text; and the cold and detached manner of historical scholarship seemed to be incompatible with implicit faith in the received interpretations of the Bible.

Biblical criticism had in fact begun under rationalistic auspices in eighteenth-century Germany. Reimarus had insisted on treating the Bible as one would treat any other historical document; and Semler and his successors had developed a discipline of biblical theology, replacing dogmatic exegesis with the literary and historical analysis of the biblical documents in their human context. Nineteenth-century studies of the Old Testament tended to treat it as the history of the people of Israel. Some scholars, such as Wellhausen, interpreted that history in terms of a development in stages from a crude belief in a tribal deity to a more ethical and universal creed. Even more important was the higher criticism of the New Testament, which commenced a new epoch in the 1830's with the rise of the school of Tübingen. The leading figure of this school was F. C. Baur, who was much influenced by Hegel. Baur saw the New Testament as the product of a tension between two tendencies in the early Church, the Petrine which regarded Jesus as the Jewish Messiah and the Pauline which preached a more universal ideal. Baur commenced a century-long discussion of the chronological order of the Gospels and questioned Paul's authorship of several of the Epistles.

The aspect of the higher criticism of the New Testament which attracted the most public attention was the attempt to reconstruct the life of Jesus in human terms. Several lives of Jesus were published in the eighteenth and nineteenth centuries which ignored or rationalized the miraculous element in the Gospel stories. Consternation was caused among the orthodox when a disciple of Baur, D. F. Strauss, published his *Leben Jesu* in 1835, embodying a direct challenge to the historical reliability of the Gospels, which Strauss regarded as mythological. The storm of protest resulted in Strauss' being deprived of his Tübingen professorship, and he eventually lost his faith.[6] A similar fate befell the French Semitic scholar Ernest Renan, whose popular *Vie de Jésus,* published in 1863, portrayed Jesus in the light of a romantic Deism.

Biblical criticism, largely a German product, was brought to England relatively late in the century, but its effects were all the more severe in a nation which was unprepared for such a treatment of the sacred books. "The Bible, and the Bible alone" was the watchword of most English Protestants, whose insularity left them unaware of the developments on the Continent. The result was an extraordinary sensitiveness to even the slightest questioning of the authenticity of the Bible—a sensitiveness exacerbated by the coincidence of biblical criticism with the challenge of Darwinism. The controversy commenced in 1860 with the publication of a book of *Essays and Reviews* by seven graduates of the University of Oxford, which was now a center of the Broad Church movement. The Essayists and Reviewers sought to acclimatize in England the critical and historical study of the Bible which had been developed by the Germans. They urged, in various ways, the free and fearless examination of the Bible in the

6 Strauss' *Leben Jesu* was translated into English by George Eliot.

light of modern scholarship and a readiness to revise traditional interpretations: "The Christian religion is in a false position when all the tendencies of knowledge are opposed to it." Instead of the open-mindedness they sought, their book was received with a storm of clerical opposition, led by Bishop Wilberforce and joined in by both evangelicals and high churchmen in a rare display of unanimity. The bishops condemned *Essays and Reviews* synodically and attempted to prosecute two of the authors. Their conviction in the church courts was reversed by the Privy Council, which, as one wit remarked, "dismissed Hell with costs, and took away from orthodox members of the Church of England their last hope of everlasting damnation."

While this conflict was still raging, another was begun by the publication of a study of the Pentateuch by a missionary bishop in Natal, John William Colenso. Colenso had been stimulated to make a critical examination of the Old Testament by questions raised by the Africans whom he sought to convert. The result of his study was the conviction that Moses was not the author of most of the Pentateuch and that many of the Bible stories were myths. In naive good faith he published his conclusion that "the Bible itself is not 'God's Word'; but assuredly 'God's Word' will be heard in the Bible, by all who will humbly and devoutly listen to it." Colenso's book, like *Essays and Reviews*, was denounced by the bishops, who called upon him to resign. A neighboring bishop deposed him and he was repudiated by nearly all his clergy. The resulting schism in Natal was not healed until a decade after Colenso's death in 1883.

Other storms followed. *Ecce Homo,* a book published anonymously in 1865 by the historian J. R. Seeley, stressed the human and ethical aspects of Jesus; widely read, it became the subject of an extensive controversy. In 1869 one of the Essayists and Reviewers, Frederick Temple, was nominated to a bishopric, and most of the bishops refused to take part in his consecration. But Temple's appointment marked the turn of the tide. He proved to be a successful bishop, and by the end of the century he became Archbishop of Canterbury. The younger generation of university graduates was increasingly sympathetic to the critical study of the Bible; indeed by 1889, with the publication of *Lux Mundi,* the lead in biblical criticism was taken by the Anglo-Catholics. The reaction to biblical criticism had been too violent to be sustained.[7]

There had been something exaggerated and even slightly comical in the reaction to biblical criticism, which showed the worst features of Victorian religiosity. Here, as in the case of the reaction against Darwinism, it seemed as if the defenders of orthodox religion were afraid of the impartial search for truth.

> There lives more faith in honest doubt,
> Believe me, than in half the creeds.

Tennyson's words are reinforced by a remark by Benjamin Jowett, one of the Essayists and Reviewers: "Doubt comes in at the window when inquiry is denied at the door." The rising generation of educated young men, retaining much of the evangelical earnestness but increasingly suspicious of a religious orthodoxy so ineptly defended, tended to drift away from formal Christianity. A novel published in 1888, Mrs. Humphry Ward's *Robert Elsmere,* tells the story of an Anglican parson who, because he can no longer believe in the creed of the Church, resigns his office and devotes the rest of his life to social service. Robert Elsmere was the type of many young men of the latter part of the century. Even within the fold of the churches, there was a shift of emphasis from doctrinal orthodoxy to the social betterment of man. More important, the role of religion in the intellectual world was much diminished. Doubt was succeeded by indifference. When Huxley debated the question of miracles with Prime Minister Gladstone in the 1890's the entire discussion seemed curiously old-fashioned. The question was no longer of interest.

---

[7] In Scotland a similar controversy took place (1876–1881) when William Robertson Smith was deprived of his professorship by the Free Kirk for his acceptance of German higher criticism.

12

Social Concerns

"Ye have the poor with you always, and whensoever ye will ye may do them good." The Christian charitable impulse persisted through the nineteenth century, strengthened by the current of religious revival; but the object of charity—"the poor"—underwent a significant change coincident with the Industrial Revolution. The vast and rapid transformation from an agrarian to an industrial society dislocated traditional social relationships and produced an entirely new class, the urban proletariat. Rootless and restive, living at the level of bare subsistence, the proletariat was only superficially a part of the civilization of the age.[1] Classical economic theory regarded such a situation as normal and irremediable; and conventional charity, with its one-to-one relationship of donor and recipient, seemed dwarfed by the expanding dimensions of the social problem. In the nineteenth century, the charitable impulse could not be meaningful or effective until it was transformed into the quest for social justice, the attempt to reorder society rather than merely to relieve individuals. The combination of the basic motive of Christian charity with a new realization of the larger social problem is the distinguishing mark of modern "social Christianity."

[1] Recent economic historians have shown that the century was not a continuous "bleak age" and that the standard of living gradually rose after the initial stages of industrialism. The benefits of industrialism, however, were not evenly diffused, and the distress of the very lowest class remained chronic.

The full realization of the dimensions of the social problem was slow in coming to churches which were, after all, rooted in the old order of society. The sudden increase of population and the mass migration to the cities brought new problems to the churches whose structure had been based on a restricted agrarian economy. There was a shortage of churches in the growing cities, and an extensive program of church building was unable to keep up with the expansion of population. In the urban centers of England in 1851 there was church accommodation for only one-third of the population, and even less in the working-class districts; in Berlin in 1880 the churches could seat only 25,000 out of 800,000 people. There was a corresponding shortage of clergy. The strain on the educational resources of the churches was great, for the need for mass education was quickly recognized; and the problem was solved only when this traditionally religious function was taken over by the state, often at the cost of a diminution of the religious content of education. Much of the failure of the churches to recognize the wider implications of the social problem may be explained by their necessary preoccupation with the task of providing the minimal services of religion to an expanding and mobile population.

Even in terms of the basic functions of religion, a large part of the working class remained unreached by Christian agencies. Although nearly everybody was baptized and professed a nominal Christianity, the level of church attendance was low—sometimes less than ten per cent. This can be partially accounted for by the shortage of churches and by the disruption of habits incident to migration; but it was also a sign of the alienation of the workers from society. In the latter part of the century the larger part of the Continental working class gave its support to revolutionary socialist movements, particularly Marxism, which were frankly anti-Christian and which served as "surrogate religions" by providing doctrines, motives for action and visions of a better world. Even where it was not Marxist, the proletariat was largely pagan. It is wrong to speak of the "loss" of the working class by the churches; much of the new proletariat had never really been Christianized. This class, which bourgeois respectability hardly deigned to notice, was the proper object of both social and religious concern.

In the Roman Catholic Church, the development of an extensive social concern was long hindered by the preoccupation of Catholics with political rather than social issues. In the traditional areas of charity, and in primary education, the religious orders did extensive and effective work. There was some anticipation of "social Catholicism" in the work of Don Bosco among urban children in Turin and in the founding of a German Catholic labor organization, the *Gesellenverein,* by Adolf Kolping. But political reaction brought about the failure of more extensive social movements in Roman Catholicism. The broad democratic sympathies of Lamennais were rejected by Gregory XVI, the hopes of social reconciliation in 1848 were quickly dashed, and Ozanam's Society of St. Vincent de Paul was suppressed by Napoleon III. It should be noted that most Roman Catholic countries, except Belgium, were relatively slow to industrialize. Only in the last third of the century, particularly after the accession of Leo XIII, did a systematic concern for the social problem become a major feature of Catholic history.

In Protestant countries responses varied more widely. Characteristically, most of these responses were essentially conservative, seeking to attach the working class to the existing order by relieving their most pressing needs. Thus the German Inner Mission, though founded on Wichern's practical insight into the problems of the workers, was limited by his characteristically Lutheran devotion to a patriarchal society under princely authority. The English evangelicals were primarily concerned with the moral rather than the material improvement of the "lower orders" and with obviating the danger of revolution. Although Lord Shaftesbury, a humanitarian of the highest order, was responsible for factory laws which improved the conditions of child and female labor, most of the legislation resulting in effective social improvements was sponsored by the secular liberals. The rival efforts of the religious and the liberal reformers melded in bringing about improvements which met the minimal needs of the working class; in England, as in almost no other country, the edge of the class struggle was blunted. The British workers remained unaffected by Marxian socialism, finding in the trade union movement, led by responsible moderates often of nonconformist origin, a means of improving their lot without revolution. Yet these efforts at collective self-improvement by the workers met with little sympathy from the churches or the upper classes.

The one Protestant movement of the first half of the century which sought to reorder society rather than merely to reform individuals was the Christian Socialism of Maurice, Kingsley, and Ludlow. Although the movement began as an immediate response to the threat of revolution in 1848, its leaders held a vision of a new society based on cooperation rather than competition. They adopted the provocative name of Christian Socialists because they believed that Christianity and socialism were both expressions of the same principle of human fellowship, that socialism was "the great Christian revolution" of the age. They sought not only to Christianize socialism but to socialize Christianity. They were able to achieve rapport with the workers and obtained much success in adult education and in the formation of voluntary societies. Their weaknesses were an overemphasis of the voluntary principle to the neglect of the necessary role of the state and a tendency to divert their energies to other fields. The movement came to an end in 1854.

The work of the Christian socialists was resumed, in the last quarter of the century, by new groups which arose from an unlikely source, the High Church party. Anglo-Catholic clergy were strikingly successful in slum parishes, and one of them, Stewart Headlam, combined ritualism with a passion for social justice which bore fruit in a vigorous organization, the Guild of St. Matthew, founded in 1877. The G.S.M. pressed for government intervention to aid the workers and often adopted flamboyant tactics in order to shock and arouse the Christian conscience. More respectable was a larger organization, the Christian Social Union, founded in 1889. The first president was the scholar-bishop Westcott, much influenced by Maurice; his successor was Charles Gore, who combined Anglo-Catholic doctrine, liberal biblical criticism, and broad social concerns. The C.S.U. concentrated on forming study groups to develop means of applying Christian principles to social conditions. The Church of England was educated to the concept that Christianity had a social mission, and by the early twentieth century Church congresses and diocesan conferences were passing resolutions in favor of a decent wage as "the first charge upon production."

Other groups with combined religious and social objectives worked more directly among the people. The Young Men's Christian Association was founded in 1844 by George Williams to enlist and to serve young men in the cities. The movement quickly spread to other countries, reaching its greatest development in the United States, and it was paralleled by the organization of Young Women's Christian Associations. The settlement house movement was another effort to bring both religion and culture to the poor, drawing young men from the universities to live and work in "settlements" in the slums. Much of modern "social work" derives from these ventures of the late nineteenth century.

From Nonconformist sources came the impetus for the crusade against drink, which was perhaps a more obvious evil in the nineteenth century than since. The "temperance" [2] movement made total abstinence a major doctrine for many evangelical Protestants and sought to obtain the legal prohibition of alcoholic beverages. Towards the end of the century the prohibition issue became the almost obsessive concern of the nonconformist churches in England and of several evangelical denominations in the United States. It is possible that this excessive stress on the liquor problem, which was more a symptom than a cause of social decay, tended to distract Christian reforming zeal from more basic economic and social issues.

2 The name "temperance" is misleading. The anti-drink movement quickly committed itself to the position of total abstinence, which is, strictly speaking, not "temperance" at all. It should be noted that this was a novel doctrine in Christianity, which had hitherto regarded alcohol (in moderation) as no different from other worldly goods. The use of wine in Christian symbolism was a source of embarrassment to abstainers, leading to the substitution of unfermented grape juice by some denominations.

The most striking effort of English Nonconformity to bring Christianity to the urban proletariat was the Salvation Army. The origins of this dramatic evangelicalism may be found in a recurrence of revivalism starting in 1859 and influenced by American examples, culminating in the revival campaigns of Dwight L. Moody in 1873–75.[3] The emphasis of the new revivalism was essentially salvationist rather than social. "City missions" were developed, especially by the Methodists. A Methodist preacher, William Booth, became an independent evangelist and opened a mission in the London slums in 1865. Here he found conventional evangelical preaching inadequate to attract the rough masses, and he gradually developed the sensational methods, notably street processions and music, and the quasi-military features which he formalized, in 1878, in the Salvation Army. The Army drew much opposition—from traditional religious elements because of its sensationalism and from secularists because if its autocratic military organization—but it enjoyed a success among the lowest class of the population which was denied to more respectable organizations.[4] Despite his primary emphasis on salvationism, Booth found it necessary to expand his work into the area of social service. His book *In Darkest England* (1890) portrayed the desperate conditions of the "submerged tenth" of the population among whom his work lay. The Salvation Army exemplifies the gradual transformation of revivalism into social work which was the necessary condition of the continued effectiveness of evangelicalism in an industrialized society.

In no country was the transformation from revivalism to social reform and the consequent development of social work institutions as extensive as in the United States. In this area there was continuous exchange of ideas and methods between America and

3 In this connection one should mention the Baptist C. H. Spurgeon, the most famous of Nonconformist preachers, who drew audiences of thousands to his Metropolitan Tabernacle.

4 The Church of England paid the Nonconformist Booth the compliment of organizing a rival Anglican body, the Church Army. Another organization which developed from the Salvation Army was the Volunteers of America, a secession led by Booth's son Ballington in protest against autocratic control from London.

Britain. Fittingly, an American coined the name for the movement: the "social gospel." The American social gospel, as preached notably by Walter Rauschenbusch, was identified with theological liberalism. It obtained its greatest influence in the first decades of the twentieth century.

In Germany the social ethics of the Ritschlians provided a theological basis for the social gospel, but the practical development of a Christian social movement was brought about by individuals who drew their inspiration from the Inner Mission. The most striking of these was Adolf Stöcker, who combined a post as court preacher with the leadership of the Berlin City Mission. A devoted servant of the Hohenzollern monarchy, Stöcker became aware of the alienation of the masses from their rulers. To counteract the rising influence of Marxism among the working class, Stöcker founded a Christian Social Labor Party in 1878, with a program of extensive labor legislation and social insurance combined with Christianity and patriotism. He was attacked by both the right and the left; the Lutheran clergy wished to confine their role to preaching and worship, and the workers were only slightly influenced by Stöcker, whose party collapsed in 1879. Undaunted, Stöcker transferred his allegiance to the Conservative party and was elected to the Reichstag. In the 1880's much of his program of social insurance was enacted by Bismarck, who was motivated partly by a Christian social concern but primarily by a desire to outbid the Marxian Socialists for the loyalty of the working class. Stöcker was one of the leaders of the Evangelical Social Congress founded in 1890; this organization, which sought to bring educated people and workingmen together, survived him and later had Harnack for its chairman. Stöcker, who had added a virulent anti-Semitism to his program,[5] was tolerated by the Conservatives until 1896, when he proposed agrarian reform. He had already been dis-

---

[5] The association of Christian socialism with anti-Semitism is a curious phenomenon which recurred in several contexts, e.g., Chesterton and Belloc in England, and Lueger in Austria. It was based on an identification of Judaism with usury and capitalism and on a sense that the Jews were an unassimilable alien element irreconcilable with the ideal of national social cohesiveness. The extreme virulence of anti-Semitism, however, had deeper and more sinister psychological roots.

missed as court preacher in 1890 by Emperor William II, who disapproved of "political pastors."

Stöcker was succeeded as leader of German social Christianity by Friedrich Naumann, a more attractive personality. Naumann was a pastor who served on the staff of the Inner Mission until 1894, when he resigned, feeling that it was too subservient to the vested interests. He then devoted himself to writing on behalf of a Christian social program. The authorities of the Evangelical Church ordered pastors to withdraw from politics, and Naumann renounced the ministry. His colleague Paul Göhre went so far as to join the Social Democratic (Marxist) party. Naumann himself joined the Liberals, and he eventually ceased to advocate a distinctively Christian position in politics.[6]

Despite its extensive network of charitable institutions, German Protestantism never developed the extensive social commitment which was characteristic of the British churches. The Lutheran tradition, sharply distinguishing the Church as a fellowship of worship from the political and social order of the world, was more powerful than the tradition of charitable works. The general opinion that pastors ought to confine themselves to spiritual affairs and eschew politics was accepted by the pastors themselves, who were firm supporters of the constituted authorities. The structure of the *Landeskirchen* afforded no scope for independent lay action. The result was that the churches became bulwarks of conservatism, and religion came to be regarded by the workers as a device to keep them submissive. The various Protestant social movements failed to halt the drift of the working class to socialism.

Two factors decisively limited the success which social Christianity was able to obtain. The first was the identification of the churches with the existing social order from which, except in England, the working class was largely alienated. In many cases the spokesmen of social Christianity accepted this identification

[6] Naumann came under the influence of the historian Rudolf Sohm, who drew a radical distinction between Christianity and the culture of the age. The effect of this was a belief that Christian morality was irrelevant to the modern political system.

and regarded their work as a religious alternative to revolutionary socialism. To a certain extent Marx was justified in calling religion the "opiate of the people." Significantly, there was an extensive rallying to religion of the middle class in the last half of the century. As the bourgeoisie, hitherto secularistic and liberal, attained the hegemony for which it had struggled, it became concerned to defend its status against more radical movements originating from the lower classes. In many countries (of which France was the most notable), religion, which had been the support of monarchy and aristocracy a half-century earlier, was now called upon to defend the supremacy of the bourgeoisie. But the working class, which by the end of the century had been generally exposed to formal education, was no longer disposed to accept with docility a program which, however sincerely humane, betrayed its upper-class origins. The quest for social reconciliation, never fully supported by the churches, was a less effective force than the class struggle.

Even more important as a factor limiting the success of social Christianity was the sheer magnitude of the social problem. The rapid expansion of population, its great mobility, and the concentration of social ills in the slums produced problems too great for the resources of any movement which relied primarily on the voluntary efforts of individuals. Only the strength and coercive power of the state could be adequate to deal with the social problem in a comprehensive manner. But the increased significance of the state meant a decline in the social importance of the churches. As the secular character of the modern state was established in the course of the nineteenth century, the relevance of the Christian religion to the social order was called into question.

13

Roman Catholicism and the Social Order

The death of Pius IX in 1878 marked the end of a phase in the history of the Roman Catholic Church. The old Pope himself had recognized this: "My system and my policies have had their day, but I am too old to change my ways. That will have to be the work of my successor." His successor was Gioacchino Pecci, who reigned as Leo XIII for a quarter of a century. The unusually long reigns of Pius and Leo provide us with convenient epochs in Church history. Whereas the ebullient Pius, after a brief flirtation with liberalism, became the staunchest of reactionaries, the grave and diplomatic Leo pursued a steady course of conciliation.

It is possible to exaggerate the differences between Pius IX and Leo XIII. By comparison with Pius, nearly any successor would have appeared liberal. In fact, Leo was no liberal.[1] The relative freedom which he allowed in intellectual affairs was predicated upon the complete triumph of ultramontanism in the previous reign. In politics and diplomacy, where he was especially successful, Leo's conciliatoriness was mixed with a firm maintenance of the rights of the Church and of the alliance of church and state. He continued to assert the necessity of the Temporal Power, thus perpetuating the Roman question and the impasse with the new

---

[1] The conclave which elected Pecci was composed of cardinals all of whom (including Pecci himself) had been created by Pius IX. This is an indication of the extent to which Pius had been able to reshape the Church during his long reign.

Kingdom of Italy, which he refused to recognize. Devout Catholics were instructed to refrain from taking part in Italian politics, and this *non expedit* was not withdrawn until the reign of the next Pope, when it became evident that the abstention of Catholics had left the field to the radicals and socialists. Leo showed his greatest originality in the field of social policy, which Pius had largely ignored; yet even here his solution to the social problem was conceived as a counterstroke to secular liberalism and socialism. The difference between Leo and Pius was one of style rather than of substance.

The difference of style was considerable. Early in his reign Leo made overtures to Bismarck which, along with the effective work of the Center party, brought about the gradual termination of the *Kulturkampf*. The period of his reign was more peaceful than that of Pius IX, and Leo established a reputation as a diplomat which enhanced his personal prestige. He showed considerable open-mindedness in intellectual affairs, particularly in the earlier part of his reign. Newman, who had been "under a cloud" in the last years of Pius, was made a Cardinal in 1879; and Leo patronized science and opened the Vatican archives to scholars.[2]

Recognizing that the education of the clergy was deficient, Leo sought to strengthen it by reviving the teaching of the great scholastic theologians, particularly St. Thomas Aquinas. In the encyclical *Aeterni Patris* (1879) he established Thomism as the norm of Catholic teaching, and he founded chairs of Thomistic studies at Catholic universities, notably at Louvain where Désiré Mercier sought to reconcile Thomism with experimental science. The Thomistic revival brought new life to Catholic philosophy. However, the deliberate choice of a medieval mode of thought has made it difficult for Catholic philosophers to communicate

[2] Cardinal Manning remarked, concerning the Vatican archives, "If the Evangelist did not conceal the sin and fall of Judas, why should we conceal the sins of bishops and other personages?" The main Vatican archives are open up to (but not including) the reign of Pius IX; some of the other Roman archives are opened after one hundred years have elapsed.

with their non-Catholic counterparts or to make effective use of contemporary developments in psychology.[3]

The most original and significant element in the policy of Leo XIII was his readiness to seek a Catholic solution to the social problems brought about by modern industrial society. In this endeavor he had been anticipated by a number of Catholics in the industrialized countries. In England Henry Edward Manning, a convert from the Oxford Movement, succeeded Wiseman as Archbishop of Westminster in 1865 and Cardinal in 1875. Wiseman's work had been to establish the Roman Catholic Church as a respectable institution in English life; Manning turned his attention to the needs of the Catholics themselves, who were largely poor Irish immigrants. He built numerous churches in the slums and extended the system of Catholic schools for the poor. Rigidly Ultramontane in his ecclesiastical principles, he described himself as a "Mosaic radical" in social policy. His popularity among the lower classes was demonstrated when his intervention proved decisive in bringing about a favorable termination to the London dock workers' strike of 1889. No Catholic prelate in Europe, with the possible exception of Bishop Mermillod of Geneva, showed a more sympathetic understanding of the aspirations of the working class.

In France the social Catholic movement remained external to the working class; it was sponsored by aristocrats and was bound up with conservative politics. Comte Albert de Mun, a royalist politician, sought to restore the stable social and religious system which had been destroyed by the Revolution and the individualistic bourgeois society which it produced. His economic ideal was the corporation or guild, characteristic of the Middle Ages. More practically, he agitated for improved working conditions and provision for the aged and disabled. He organized workers' "circles" or clubs under aristocratic sponsorship. However, he

[3] Two psychologist-philosophers, William James and Henri Bergson, writing around the turn of the century, asserted the psychological validity of religious experience. Although they were influential among younger lay intellectuals, their work was not received sympathetically by the Church.

failed to understand that the French working class had long since accepted the Revolution, whose results were irreversible. At a later date more democratic social Catholic movements began to develop, and some useful work was done by study groups and youth organizations, but they were always held back by the reactionary politics of the majority of French Catholics. The most ambitious effort of French social Catholicism was an enthusiastic if somewhat vague youth movement known as *Sillon*. Led by Marc Sangnier, it combined a spiritual revival with social and democratic aspirations. Caught in the struggle between the Church and the Republic, the movement was crushed by Pius X in 1910 on the ground of its independence of ecclesiastical authority. In general, French social Catholicism was little more than a beautiful dream.

In Austria a largely aristocratic group led by Baron von Vogelsang supported a corporatist program similar to that of de Mun; but the effective leader of social Catholicism was a lawyer of peasant origin, Karl Lueger, who organized a Christian Social party in the 1880's and won extensive support from the workers. As Burgomaster of Vienna he was a successful municipal reformer, and his party enacted much legislation on behalf of the working class. Unfortunately, Austrian social Catholicism was heavily infected with anti-Semitism, identifying the evils of both capitalism and socialism with the Jews; and Lueger must be reckoned among the forerunners of Hitler.

The most important of the precursors of Leo XIII in social Catholicism was Bishop Ketteler of Mainz, aristocrat, Ultramontane, and leader of the German clergy at the time of the *Kulturkampf*. Ketteler's *Christianity and the Labor Question* (1864) formulated a Catholic program of social reform, including improvement of wages and hours and opposition to child and female labor. A Catholic labor movement was organized and, although the socialists dominated the larger trade unions, the German Catholic workers showed less tendency to abandon the faith than did the French. The Center party, which remained the political expression of German Catholicism, transcended class distinctions to an unusual degree and supported Bismarck's program of social legislation.

In general, the social Catholicism of the Continent was closely related to the continuing opposition of the Church to the results of the Revolution. One of those results was the secular liberalism of the middle class, with whose anti-clerical program the Church had been in conflict throughout the century. The laissez-faire doctrines of classical economic liberalism had taken less firm root in the largely agricultural countries of Catholic Europe than in the Protestant North, and it was easier for Catholics than for individualistic Protestants to accept the principle of state intervention in economic affairs. Further, since an active social policy would in effect reduce the economic supremacy of the middle class, it could attract support from the aristocracy, which was in many countries the mainstay of the Church, and which tended to idealize the stratified society of pre-industrial, pre-Revolutionary days. And at the same time the demonstration of social concern by Church and state would tend to counteract a menace feared by both the aristocracy and the bourgeoisie, the rise of Marxian socialism. If the working class were to form organizations of its own, it was desirable that they should be formed under the aegis of the Church, which would blunt their revolutionary edge. Yet social Catholicism was not merely a calculated attempt to undercut liberalism and socialism. At its best, it was a genuine effort to achieve social harmony, a mutual respect of classes, such as was (perhaps mistakenly) believed to have existed in the medieval Ages of Faith. The Roman Catholic Church refused to accept the idea of the class struggle and adhered instead to the dream of social unity.

All these elements of social Catholicism may be found in judicious balance in the great social pronouncements of Leo XIII. The most important of these was the encyclical *Rerum novarum* (1891), in which Leo adopted the position of Ketteler and placed the Church on the side of social justice. "The condition of the working classes is the pressing question of the hour," he said, and some remedy was urgently needed for the laboring poor who

suffered under "a yoke little better than that of slavery itself."
Leo condemned the proposed remedy of socialism. He argued
that the right of private property is inviolable and the inequality
of fortunes inevitable. The ideal was the harmony of classes
under the auspices of religion. Workers must respect property,
fulfill contracts and avoid violence; employers must respect in
every worker "his dignity and worth as a man and as a Christian." Leo asserted the principle of the "fair wage," adequate "to
support a frugal and well-behaved wage-earner" and to allow
him the prospect of bettering his condition and acquiring property. The state may intervene, if necessary, to provide that "dis-
tributive" justice be done to the working class, although it must
respect the prior rights of the individual and the family. The
workers may form associations of their own, such as the medieval
guilds, and the state should not deny the right of association.
Catholic workingmen were encouraged to form specifically Catholic associations.

Contemporaries were impressed, and even stunned, by the
vigor with which Leo proclaimed the need for justice for the
working class. He had clearly rejected the doctrine of laissez-faire
and asserted the propriety of state intervention in the economic
sphere. The justification of the right of workers to form unions
followed closely upon his refusal, in 1887, to condemn the
Knights of Labor in America. These positions were bold and
striking in their day. At the present time, a careful reader of
Rerum novarum would be more impressed by the strong defense
of private property, the assumption of social inequality, the limitations on the activity of the state and the medievalism implicit
in the idealization of the guilds. The Catholic trade unions
which Leo envisioned rarely attained much success, but the
"Catholic Action" of the twentieth century finds its origin in this
encyclical. Leo's work has been the foundation of subsequent
Catholic social thought, to which the term "Christian democracy" has often been applied. This term received Leo's rather
qualified endorsement in the encyclical *Graves de communi*
(1901).

The balanced social pronouncements of Leo XIII were made

in a political context which may best be described as moderate conservatism. By the late nineteenth century, constitutional parliamentary governments were becoming normal in Europe, and the working classes were being admitted in varying degrees to the suffrage. A master politician, Leo accepted the new constitutional order; a born aristocrat, he never accepted the principle of democracy. In a series of encyclicals,[4] Leo declared that the Church was indifferent to particular forms of government, including the democratic, but he insisted that civil power comes from God and not from the consent of men. He continued to oppose the separation of church and state and freedom of thought and religion. At the outset of his reign Leo had said, "I desire that modern society should end by reconciling itself sooner or later to the *Syllabus,* by understanding all its aims." The difference between Pius IX and Leo XIII was that the former emphasized the "thesis," the absolute claims of the Church, and the latter preferred to stress the "hypothesis," the practical adjustment to the actual situation.

The severest test of Leo's policies came in France. The empire of Napoleon III had collapsed in the defeat of 1870, and a republic was proclaimed. However, a majority of the deputies elected in 1871 were monarchists, and it seemed likely that a monarchy would be restored. The clergy and devout Catholics were overwhelmingly in favor of a monarchy. The monarchists, however, were divided into two camps: the legitimists, who supported the grandson of Charles X and the principle of absolutism, and the Orleanists, who supported the grandson of Louis Philippe and the idea of constitutional monarchy. Because of this division, the monarchists missed their opportunity, and France became a republic by default. Between 1877 and 1879 the republican Left—

---

[4] The device of the encyclical (general letter) was extensively employed by both Pius IX and Leo XIII for doctrinal and moral instruction, setting forth authoritatively the position of the Church. Among Leo's more significant encyclicals, not otherwise mentioned here, are *Quod apostolici muneris* (1878), *Diuturnum illud* (1881), *Libertas* (1888), and *Sapientiae Christianae* (1890).

the secular liberals and their radical allies—came into power, united behind a program which was not merely anti-monarchical but anti-clerical. Their leader Gambetta proclaimed their motto: "Clericalism, there is the enemy!" The Church was to suffer for its alliance with the defeated monarchists.

The program of the anti-clericals was to reduce the influence of the Church on French life by striking at the religious orders and by removing the Church from public education. In 1880 the Jesuits were expelled and other religious orders were required to apply for legal authorization; some of the orders, refusing to apply, were suppressed. More important were the "laic laws," authored by Jules Ferry, secularizing public education. In 1880 the influence of ecclesiastics on educational administration was eliminated, reversing the effect of the Falloux Law of 1850, and Catholic institutions were forbidden to call themselves universities or to grant degrees. State schools were established for the education of girls, hitherto a Church monopoly. In 1881 public education was made free, in 1882 religious teaching was eliminated from state schools, and in 1886 members of religious orders were removed from the teaching staffs. The basis was thus laid for the system of secular schools which has since dominated French education, despite the efforts of the Church to establish a parallel system of Catholic schools. In a similar conflict at this time in Belgium, a vigorous Catholic political response overcame the secularists in the election of 1884; but the French Catholics, still blindly committed to the hopeless monarchist cause, were repeatedly defeated.

The accession of Leo XIII had virtually coincided with the secularist offensive against the Church in France, and for several years Leo's diplomatic efforts were frustrated by the combined forces of republican anti-clericalism and Catholic monarchism. After the failure in 1889 of the Boulangist movement against the republic, which many Catholics had supported, Leo judged the moment right to urge French Catholics to come to terms with the new political order.[5] This attempt to reconcile the Catholics to

[5] Leo was assisted in his conciliatory policy by Cardinal Rampolla, Secretary of State since 1887.

the republic is known as *ralliement*. It was begun in 1890 by a speech of Cardinal Lavigerie, inspired by the Pope, openly endorsing the Republic. So unwilling were French Catholics, including most of the hierarchy, to follow this lead that Leo himself had to intervene, first by an interview in which he stated that "the republican is as legitimate a form of government as others," and finally with the encyclical *Au milieu des sollicitudes* (1892), declaring that Catholics must accept the constituted authorities and should take part in the Republic, working from within to rectify its faults. Although many Catholics stubbornly maintained their monarchism, there emerged a significant group of Catholics loyal to the Republic (*ralliés*). However, *ralliement* had come too late to overcome either the anti-clericalism of the Left or the continued attraction of the Catholics to the lost causes of the Right.

The Dreyfus case of the late 1890's brought about the failure of the *ralliement* and the final rupture of church and state in France. Captain Dreyfus, a Jew, was unjustly convicted of treason on evidence forged by other officers. Despite mounting evidence in Dreyfus' favor, the army refused to reverse his condemnation. The army was supported by the monarchists, who hoped to use the case to discredit the republic, by the anti-Semites, and by a majority of the Catholics. The defense of truth and justice was thus left to the republicans, who turned the Dreyfus case into a battle for the soul of France. Dreyfus was pardoned in 1899 and fully rehabilitated in 1906, by which time the facts of the case had been established and the army and its right-wing allies were discredited. The republicans, under increasingly radical leadership, were once again victorious and organized a government of "republican defense" to consolidate their victory. Although the principal responsibility for the affair rested with the army officers and the anti-Semites, it was the Church which had to suffer the consequences.

The first blows were struck, as before, at the religious orders and Catholic schools. A Law of Associations in 1901 required religious orders to obtain specific legislative authorization and forbade unauthorized orders to operate schools. In 1902 a more radical ministry, under the renegade ex-seminarian Emile Combes, took office, and "republican defense" was transformed into an offensive against the Church. The majority of orders were refused authorization, many of the communities were dispersed in 1903, and a large number of Catholic schools were closed. In 1904 all members of religious orders were forbidden to teach.

The next stage was a direct conflict with the Papacy. In 1903 Leo XIII died. His successor was the saintly Pius X, an admirable priest but inexperienced as a diplomat. Pius chose as his Secretary of State the brilliant but extremely conservative Merry del Val. There were several quarrels over the nomination of bishops, but the decisive incident was the state visit of the President of France to Rome in 1904. The President paid his respects to the King of Italy but not to the Pope. Pius X was offended, especially because he still maintained his claim to the Temporal Power and regarded the King of Italy as a usurper in Rome, and Merry del Val sent a stiff note of protest. The French government thereupon broke diplomatic relations with the Vatican.

The final stage of the conflict, toward which the republicans had long been tending, was the abrogation of the Concordat of 1801 and the separation of church and state. The Law of Separation (December, 1905) annulled the Concordat by the unilateral act of the French Parliament. The state withdrew its financial support (except for some pensions) from the Roman Catholic Church, as well as from Protestants and Jews, and church buildings were declared to be state property. Provision was made for the use of the buildings and the continuing support of religion by voluntary associations of the faithful (*associations cultuelles*). In return for the loss of its state support and legal privileges, the Church regained complete internal autonomy and the Pope was free to appoint bishops as he chose.

Although the French bishops were prepared reluctantly to adjust to the new law, Pius X, by the encyclical *Vehementer* (1906), condemned the separation of church and state and forbade the organization of the *associations cultuelles* on the ground that the administration of the Church should not be entrusted to laymen. All attempts at compromise were refused by the intransigent Pope. Working arrangements were informally reached by which the Church continued to function and to use its former buildings, but the legal status of the Church remained insecure and its work was hampered for several years. The conflict of church and state continued until the outbreak of World War I in 1914, when all parties united in a "sacred union" against the national enemy. After the war the religious issue appeared less acute, and a *modus vivendi* was arranged in the early 1920's.

The result of the long church-state conflict was a substantial de-Christianization of France. The Church lost the prestige which had accrued from its former connection with the state and, although many Catholic schools survived, the younger generation largely received its education in state schools from which religious teaching had been excluded. On the other hand, the Church had regained its freedom of action, the authority of the Pope was strengthened, and Roman Catholicism, liberated from reliance on the state, was able to devote itself more fully to its religious mission. That this was not a useless freedom was shown by the growth of Catholic action in the twentieth century. Nonetheless, the strength of the French Church rested upon a very specific social base: the upper classes rather than the workers, peasants in certain regions rather than urban populations, and women rather than men. The devotion of the devout was unchanged by the vicissitudes of the Church, but the religious habits of the indifferent masses had been severely shaken in the century since the Revolution.

14

Modernism, and After

Throughout the nineteenth century Christianity had been confronted with intellectual challenges, as received doctrines came into real or apparent conflict with the latest developments in scientific thought. Throughout the century there were movements whose purpose was to reconcile religion with science by some degree of acceptance of scientific criticism. In the German universities the Protestant faculties enjoyed great freedom and were able to adopt advanced liberal views; in Britain the history of liberal theology was a series of crises, each marking a slight advance in freedom of interpretation; in the Roman Catholic world liberal doctrines were propounded only occasionally and were crushed by the heavy hand of authority.

Confronted by evolutionary science and historical criticism, which particularly challenged received views of the Old Testament, the liberal theologians of the mid-century had sought to preserve the basic dogmas of Christianity by disengaging them from the struggle, by asserting that the doctrines of the Christian faith were not affected by the disproof of biblical inerrancy. This task was rendered difficult by the fact that dogmas—the verbal formulae which express basic articles of faith—were couched in language which was becoming increasingly difficult to reconcile with scientific views. Confronted by further developments in criticism, notably the more searching analysis of the New Testament, and by new studies in the psychology of belief, a number of those

seeking to reconcile science and religion at the end of the century
began to distinguish between the substance of faith and its dogmatic formulation. The essence of the Christian faith, they
found, was the internal experience of the believer which no intellectual formula could adequately express; dogmas were therefore
not immutable and must be modified to conform with the results
of scientific criticism. This is the characteristic note of those
movements which came to be known as Modernist.

Modernism is difficult to define because it never emerged as an
organized movement with a clearly stated program. Rather, the
Modernists were individuals who, in the effort to adjust the expression of the Christian religion to the needs of science, showed
certain common tendencies: developmentalism, immanentism,
and pragmatism. The developmental approach—the tendency to
regard the history of the Christian faith as an evolutionary process—gained renewed strength with the progress of New Testament criticism and with liberal Protestant studies of the origins
of the Church. In the hands of some critics the result of such
studies was a secular intellectualism, and the Modernists were to
be accused of this fault. It would be more accurate to say that the
Modernists were anti-intellectual, or "fideist," in their approach,
for they sought to detach the essence of faith from any verbal or
rational formulation which might be subject to destruction at
the hands of scientific criticism. They found the Christian faith
to be immanent in the interior nature and aspirations of the
human individual.[1] Influenced by the intuitionism of Henri
Bergson and the pragmatism of William James, they held that
religious truth was to be found not in any intellectual statement
but in the inner experience of each man. Such an attitude allowed the Modernists to be quite free in accepting the results of
secular science without (as they thought) abandoning the Christian faith in its properly religious sphere. In Modernism a superficial rationalism concealed an almost mystical subjectivism. This
combination placed them in a position to conduct a potentially

[1] This "immanentism" may be traced to Maurice Blondel, whose book
L'Action (1893) argued that, without relying on transcendentalist arguments,
it could be shown that human nature itself presupposed the supernatural.

useful dialogue with the scientific critics of Christianity. On the other hand, the abandonment of fixed doctrinal standards and the implicit denial of the rationality of faith raised doubts as to whether the Modernists were suitable defenders of the Christian religion. In throwing overboard the excess intellectual baggage of Christianity, it was asked, what had they left?

The Modernist movement was most prominent within the Roman Catholic Church, but there were Protestant counterparts which deserve to be noticed. In England the publication of *Lux Mundi* (1889) revealed the presence of a group of liberal Anglo-Catholics, led by Charles Gore, who combined biblical criticism with a deep devotion to the Church and its sacraments. The next generation of liberal Anglo-Catholics went further than Gore; in a symposium entitled *Foundations* (1912) they suggested that the historicity of the New Testament could be replaced by the appeal to Christian experience. In Germany the liberal school of which Harnack was the chief may be regarded as a counterpart of Modernism; it distinguished the basically simple message of Jesus from the "Hellenic" intellectual accretions which had been superimposed upon it in the course of the evolution of dogma. Harnack, however, was criticized by the Roman Catholic Modernists for disregarding the necessary role of the Church. The most direct link between Protestant and Catholic Modernism was Auguste Sabatier, dean of the Protestant theological faculty at Paris, whose theory of critical symbolism treated dogmas as provisional symbolic expressions of religious experience. The substance of faith was distinguished from the formulae of belief.

Roman Catholic Modernism would seem to have had a precursor in the Liberal Catholicism of Döllinger, Acton, and Simpson, but in fact there was no connection between the two movements. The Liberal Catholics had been crushed by 1870, and critical studies within Roman Catholicism did not revive until the accession of Leo XIII, whose early years seemed to promise a new freedom for Catholic intellectuals. The Catholic Institute of Paris became a center at which the revival of intellectual activity among the clergy came into contact with the contemporary spirit of criticism. Here Louis Duchesne, professor of church history, developed a school of critical scholars who boldly attacked received traditions with the weapons of historical research. Duchesne himself was no Modernist, but his favorite pupil, Alfred Loisy, dealt directly with biblical questions and challenged the doctrine of the inerrancy of the Bible. Loisy was to move toward an increasingly radical position, abandoning belief in the creed while retaining his love for the Church and his position as a priest. By the early 1890's Loisy had become an object of suspicion to the more conservative theologians.

By this time the relative liberalism of the early years of Leo XIII was fading, and the "integralists" (as the conservatives were called) were ready for a counter-attack against Modernist tendencies even before these had fully manifested themselves. Loisy was dismissed from the Catholic Institute in 1893. When the Rector of the Institute sought to defend Loisy in an article on the biblical question, he was met with a direct response from Rome. The encyclical *Providentissimus Deus* (1893) asserted the fundamentalist doctrine of biblical inerrancy: "For all the books which the Church receives as sacred and canonical are written wholly and entirely, with all their parts, at the dictation of the Holy Spirit." [2] In 1902, Leo established a Biblical Commission to supervise Catholic biblical studies.

Another sign of the reaction against liberal and modernist tendencies was the condemnation of a tendency which was given the inaccurate name of "Americanism." A number of French Catholics, devoted to *ralliement* and seeking to reconcile the Church to modern society, found their model in America, where the "free Church in a free State" was a reality. They could find in such Americans as Cardinal Gibbons, Archbishop Ireland, and Father Isaac Hecker statements proclaiming the virtues of freedom and the need to present Catholicism in a modern fashion. A French translation of a biography of Hecker presented these ideas in a provocative manner. The response was a Papal letter,

[2] To appreciate the revival of Catholic biblical scholarship in recent decades, *Providentissimus Deus* and the subsequent rulings of Pius X should be compared with the encyclicals of Pius XII, *Divino Afflante Spiritu* (1943) and *Humani Generis* (1951).

Testem benevolentiae (1899), criticizing opinions "going under the name of Americanism," such as the extolling of the active virtues over the passive and reliance upon individual inspiration rather than ecclesiastical guidance. Included in the letter was a condemnation of the idea that the Church, in order to convert outsiders, should modify its doctrines to suit the ideas of the age. "Americanism" has been called the "phantom heresy" because, as the American bishops hastened to assure the Pope, it had no formal adherents in America. In fact the Pope was denouncing French ideas, political rather than theological, and the episode should be viewed in the light of the failure of *ralliement* and the revival of intransigence. Americanist opinions were part of the complex of ideas concerned with the reconciliation of the Church to modern thought of which Modernism was also a part; and the condemnation of Americanism may be regarded as one of the first blows in the struggle against Modernism.

The final struggle did not take place until after the death of Leo XIII, and in the interval Modernist ideas spread among the Catholic intellectual elite of several countries. In Germany Hermann Schell of Würzburg published a book in 1897 on *Catholicism as Principle of Progress* which was placed on the Index. A link among liberal thinkers of several nations was the German-born Baron Friedrich von Hügel, domiciled in England. He was a close friend of George Tyrrell, a convert from Anglicanism who had become a Jesuit priest. Tyrrell became dissatisfied with scholastic thought and came to the conclusion that theology was not the statement of unchangeable truths but must be the dynamic expression of the living experience of the Church, expressed in contemporary terms. There was also a Modernist movement in Italy, more political than theological, headed by the democratic priest Romolo Murri and the senator Antonio Fogazzaro. In France, Loisy, who was temporarily in retirement, received support from the priest Lucien Laberthonnière and the pragmatist philosopher Edouard LeRoy.

In 1902 Loisy returned to public activity with a book, *The Gospel and the Church*, a critique of Harnack's liberal Protestantism. Loisy argued that Jesus preached not a merely personal trust in God but an objective messianic kingdom; the institutional Church with its dogmas was the necessary form in which the Gospel had to be preserved and developed. This was a promising line of Catholic apologetic, especially since liberal Protestantism was just then coming under attack by the rediscovery of New Testament eschatology; but Loisy's developmental approach to the history of dogma involved a rejection of biblical inerrancy and scholastic orthodoxy. About this "little book," as Loisy called it, the struggle broke out anew.

At this juncture the aged Leo XIII died. His successor, Pius X, was a "spiritual" rather than a "political" Pope: a saintly man (he was canonized in 1954), at heart a simple parish priest, he had shown himself an admirable bishop, but he had neither experience in politics nor interest in intellectual affairs.[3] Nonetheless, guided only by his conscience as a priest and with a firm conviction of the authority of his office, he did not hesitate to take rigid positions which made his reign one of crisis and turmoil. Pius X has been described as a mixture of a village curate and an archangel with a fiery sword. He lacked the dexterity of Leo XIII, and the result was the final rupture between church and state in France and the definitive stage of the conflict with Modernism. From the first, Pius showed himself to be the Pope of the integralists. Leo's Biblical Commission had included some moderates, but Pius replaced them with conservatives, and late in 1903 five of Loisy's books were placed on the Index. In 1906 Tyrrell was expelled from the Society of Jesus; works by Laberthonnière and LeRoy were condemned; the Biblical Commission issued a series of rulings enforcing a literalist interpretation of the Bible; and in 1907 Murri was suspended from his priestly functions.

In the summer of 1907 came the definitive condemnation of Modernism. The decree *Lamentabili,* issued by the Inquisition

[3] Pius' primary interest was in spiritual affairs; his motto was "to restore all things in Christ." He worked for the spiritual improvement of the clergy, revised the regulations concerning matrimony, promoted frequent communion and the admission of young children to the sacrament, and encouraged the revival of Gregorian chant. Under Pius X was begun the codification of canon law which was completed in 1918.

with the express sanction of the Pope, was a new syllabus of errors condemning sixty-five propositions drawn mainly from the works of Loisy. Then the encyclical *Pascendi,* issued by Pius himself, condemned Modernism systematically, describing it as a conspiracy to subvert the Church and giving an outline of its philosophy: the denial of rational proofs of religion, the doctrine of "vital immanence," the assertion that revelation was to be found in the inner consciousness of man apart from the Church, the denial of the supernatural in history, and the insistence that the Church must accommodate her teaching to modern opinions. The Pope's picture of a composite Modernist was almost a caricature of the movement, which lacked the systematic and conspiratorial character that was imputed to it; but the condemnation was nonetheless decisive. It was followed by a persecution of remarkable severity. A number of individual Modernists and their works were condemned. In 1910 the Pope required that virtually all priests take an anti-Modernist oath which included an acceptance of the rational proofs for the existence of God and an assertion of the immutability of dogma. "Councils of vigilance" were set up in every diocese to ferret out Modernists. An atmosphere of suspicion prevailed within the Church until the accession of Benedict XV in 1914.

If the condemnation of Modernism was excessive in its severity, it was also effective. By 1910 the movement was crushed, dying with barely a whimper. Tyrrell, indeed, issued a protest, and an Italian priest, Ernesto Buonaiuti, was the anonymous author of *The Program of Modernism,* a thorough critique of *Pascendi.* However, the fact that Modernism was not an organized movement but merely an intellectual tendency of certain individuals prevented the formation of any systematic resistance. Loisy had virtually removed himself from the Church and was formally expelled in 1908; Tyrrell, excommunicated in 1907, died in 1909; others who refused to submit were excommunicated; and, except for the clandestine resistance of an ineffective few, the remaining Modernists made their submission. At first sight the collapse of Modernism seems surprising, but it should be remembered that it was a movement only of a small intellectual elite with no popular support, and it was crushed before it had even had time fairly to present its case.

The entire affair was a tragedy not only for the Modernists but for the Church. Some Modernists had clearly taught formal heresy, particularly the assertion that dogmas were not immutable, and Pius X and the integralists were sincere in their determination to preserve the purity of the deposit of faith; but the reaction was excessively severe and had overtones of panic rather than of majesty. There was little appreciation of the intellectual difficulties of Catholic scholars and no sensitivity to the context in which the Modernists had operated. Modernism was a response to developments in scholarship emanating largely from non-Catholic sources; the Modernists were engaged in a work of apologetics, the only alternative to which was to ignore these developments entirely at the cost of breaking contact with modern thought. It is characteristic of apologetics that the argument is couched in the language of the adversary rather than in terms congenial to the position being defended. Hence apologetics tends to verge on heresy; and to those who are more concerned with the position defended than with the effectiveness of the defense, the most successful apologetic may appear the most objectionable. This was the problem with which liberal Roman Catholic thinkers had been beset throughout the century. The Roman Catholic response to the nineteenth century was a closing of ranks behind the traditional positions, ever more firmly asserted. The Modernists had carried their accommodation to the modern world too far, and the reaction was correspondingly severe. The condemnation of Modernism committed the Church for more than a generation to the position of *Pascendi* and *Lamentabili*, with very serious results for Catholic scholarship, especially in biblical and scientific fields. Yet it is possible to exaggerate the significance of this reaction. The *aggiornamento* of John XXIII was only half a century away.

By a curious irony, the scholarship of the German universities, which had provided the basis of the liberal theologies of the nineteenth century, produced in the twentieth century the most powerful criticism of religious liberalism. Liberal theology—a Protestant tendency of which Modernism was the most advanced Roman Catholic counterpart—was the result of reading back into the biblical and patristic eras the sentimental, ethical, historical, and progressive outlooks of the nineteenth century. Many of these assumptions did not carry over into the twentieth century, particularly after the shattering experience of World War I. Even before the war, there was beginning a significant shift in criticism and theology. Not by the decrees of ecclesiastical authority, but by the very methods of scholarship that had engendered it, liberal theology was dealt the severest blows it ever received.

The nineteenth-century critics had sought to ascertain the "historical Jesus," as distinguished from the traditional accounts of Christ. Their "lives of Jesus" had tended to portray Him in their own image, as a teacher of love rather than of dogma, as the builder of an ethical community rather than as the Messiah whose return was imminent. A great stumbling-block for this interpretation was the fact that the biblical account gives clear indications that the outlook of Jesus and the early disciples was essentially Messianic, other-worldly, and eschatological. The boldest of the critics were prepared to dismiss these passages as spurious. Reacting against this, Johannes Weiss' monograph, *The Preaching of Jesus on the Kingdom of God* (1892), asserted that the eschatological element in the Gospels must be taken seriously, producing a picture of Jesus far different from that of Ritschl or Harnack. The "lives of Jesus" were subjected to a devastating critique by Albert Schweitzer in *The Quest of the Historical Jesus* [4] (1906), which argued that Jesus could not be portrayed in terms congenial to the modern mind. It appeared that the "historical Jesus" was not the Jesus of the nineteenth-

[4] The original title was *From Reimarus to Wrede*. Reimarus, an eighteenth-century founder of biblical criticism, took an eschatological approach which was ignored by his successors; Wrede was the most recent and thoroughgoing of the liberals. It might be noted that Schweitzer was reluctant to accept the theological implications of his own conclusions, being inclined to the "ethic of active love" rather than eschatology. His departure for Africa as a medical missionary left his critical work incomplete.

century historians, that He must be regarded in ' theological rather than merely ethical terms.

The optimistic presuppositions of liberal theology, with its vision of a rational and ethical Christendom, were shattered by the shocking experience of World War I. There was, after the war, a sharp reaction against both the liberalism and the "culture-Protestantism" of the previous century, against all tendencies which too closely identified Christianity with a modern world which had gone mad. At this juncture came the rediscovery of the thought of Kierkegaard, with his radical and paradoxical critique of the nineteenth century and its churches. The distaste for abstract theorizing, the new sense of evil in man, and the need to identify and assert personal existence in an irrational and meaningless world gave a great vogue to "existentialist" [5] doctrines. The combination of the post-war reaction and the revival of Kierkegaard brought about the rise of the "crisis theology" which has become as characteristic of the twentieth century as liberal theology was of the nineteenth.

The signal for this theological revolution was given by Karl Barth's *Commentary on the Epistle to the Romans* (1919). Barth, a Swiss pastor, had become disillusioned with liberal theology; from Kierkegaard, to whose revival he contributed, he learned that the Christian religion must be not the service of man but the worship of a God who was "wholly other," beyond the comprehension of human intelligence, approachable only by the "leap into the void" which is faith. Returning to the Reformation for his inspiration, Barth urged that theology must rest itself on the Bible, the revelation of the Word of God, always to be regarded with awe and obedience, meaningful only in the context of faith. Barth's emphasis was always on the living God, sitting in judgment over man, speaking with authority, at once the source and the object of faith. Barth's apparent denigration of human capacities was a corrective and a protest against a

[5] Perhaps the most convenient definition of the much-abused word "existential" is that of Karl Heim: "A proposition or truth is said to be existential when I cannot apprehend or assent to it from the standpoint of a mere spectator but only on the ground of my total existence."

liberalism which had overemphasized the role of reason, ignored the concept of sin, and disregarded the infinite distinction between God and man. "One can *not* speak of God simply by speaking of man in a loud voice." It was a complete repudiation of the ideas of immanence and progress so popular in the nineteenth century.

This new (or rather, newly-presented) theology has been called the theology of crisis, because it taught that man and his religion stand always under the *Krisis*, the judgment of God. It has also, particularly in its existentialist forms, been called "dialectical theology," because it employs the method of statement and counter-statement to emphasize the paradoxes that are at the heart of Christianity. Perhaps the best name is the "theology of the Word of God," because of Barth's central emphasis on God speaking and man listening. Barth himself has not been the sole proponent of this theology, which in many of its manifestations has represented a return to confessional orthodoxy.

The significance of Karl Barth for the study of nineteenth-century religious thought is that, as the greatest theologian of the early twentieth century, he stands at the opposite pole from Schleiermacher, the first and perhaps the greatest of the liberal theologians. The century which had begun with Schleiermacher and Baur ended with Schweitzer and Barth. It was an antithesis worthy of Hegel. If in any way the theology of the twentieth century is richer than that of its predecessor, it is because of the process of debate by which the nineteenth century both produced and corrected its doctrines.

15

The Eastern Orthodox Churches

The history of the Orthodox Churches of Eastern Europe and the Near East is an exception to the general pattern of church history in the nineteenth century. The Eastern Churches were only slightly affected by the great revolutions of western Europe, nor did they experience as significant a movement of revival. Rather, their history was shaped by their traditional and essentially non-Western heritage, ultimately derived from the Byzantine empire, and by the social and political circumstances of the successors of Byzantium, the Ottoman Turks and the Muscovite Russians. The hallmarks of Eastern Orthodoxy were a tenacious resistance to alien elements, an emphasis on the formal elements of religion (hierarchy and liturgy), and a close and subordinate relationship to the state. In the nineteenth century, the Eastern Orthodox churches had an undramatic history with relatively few major developments in religious thought or practice; for them, the revolution was yet to come.

Two major divisions of Eastern Orthodoxy are to be observed.[1]

[1] A third category of Eastern churches should also be noted: the non-orthodox churches derived from the great schisms of the fourth and fifth centuries, such as the Nestorians and Monophysites. These communities survived in the Near East as "fossils" (to use Toynbee's term) amidst a predominantly Moslem population. Some of them, notably the Lebanese Maronites and the Cilician Armenians, were reconciled to the Roman Catholic Church and formed "Uniate" churches, subordinate to Rome but retaining their own hierarchy and liturgy. It was to these Uniate and non-orthodox churches that most of the nineteenth-century missionary efforts in the Near East were directed.

The first comprises the Greek and Slavic churches of the Near East and Balkans, subject to the Ottoman Empire, and placed under the primacy of the Oecumenical Patriarch of Constantinople. The other and larger division was the Russian Orthodox Church, independently organized and associated with the Russian state. Much of the history of modern Orthodoxy is to be explained by the fact that the only independent Orthodox state was Russia and the other Orthodox churches had a long history of subjection to a non-Christian government.

The subjection of the Greek Orthodox Church dated from the fifteenth century. The Turks were at once oppressive and tolerant to their non-Moslem subjects, taxing them heavily yet allowing them religious freedom. Indeed, the Turks chose to organize their subjects as semi-autonomous communities (the *millet* system) on a religious rather than ethnic basis, with the religious leader of each community responsible for his followers. All the Orthodox Christians of the empire, whether Greek or Slavic, were placed under the authority of the Greek Patriarch of Constantinople. The power of the Greek clergy was thus increased by their Turkish masters, but at the same time they were forced to become the instruments of the oppression of their co-religionists. The Greek community of Constantinople, known as the Phanariots,[2] provided agents for both the Patriarch and the Sultan and became powerful throughout the empire. In the eighteenth century they won the governorships of the Rumanian provinces and secured the suppression of the Serbian and Bulgarian patriarchates, placing the control of these churches in Greek hands. The Phanariot Greeks had found in the *millet* system a means of dominating the non-Greek Christians of the Balkans through the power of the Patriarchate of Constantinople.

The Ottoman empire in the nineteenth century was the "sick man of Europe," decaying internally and threatened by the expansionist tendencies of the European powers, especially Russia. The situation of the Christian minorities gave some European states an opportunity to intervene even in the internal affairs of the empire: France had long held the right to protect Roman

2 The Greek quarter of Constantinople was known as the Phanar.

Catholics in Turkey, and now Russia claimed a protectorate over the Orthodox. The religious communities were used as pawns in great-power politics; in one instance a squabble over the Holy Places led to a major war, the Crimean War (1853–1856). Only the inability of the great powers to agree on a division of its territories saved Turkey from complete dismemberment. Even so, the Ottoman empire lost many of its provinces, especially in the Balkans, where several new states were formed. This process was due not only to external pressures but also to the development of nationalistic movements among the Balkan peoples. Nationalism was the one western ideology which proved congenial to the East. It dealt fatal blows to the multi-national Ottoman empire, to the *millet* system, and to the hegemony of the Patriarchate of Constantinople.

The first national revolt took place in Greece, which had maintained extensive commercial and cultural contacts with the West. The revolt, which began in 1821, was successful only through foreign intervention. The Sultan, holding the Patriarch responsible for the conduct of his *millet,* ordered him to be beheaded and his body desecrated. The newly-independent Greek state, only half the size of present-day Greece, found it inconvenient to be ecclesiastically dependent on a Patriarch of Constantinople who was still a Turkish subject. In 1833 the Church of Greece declared itself "autocephalous" ("self-headed" or autonomous), governed by a Holy Synod of bishops appointed by the King. The Patriarch eventually recognized this arrangement in 1850, and every subsequent addition of territory to Greece was accompanied by the withdrawal of further dioceses from the obedience of Constantinople, although formal communion was maintained. Under the Greek state the clergy lost much of its political importance and many monasteries were dissolved, but the quality of the life of the Church improved throughout the century.

Nationalistic movements elsewhere in the Balkans brought about similar results: independence from the Turks and a withdrawal of obedience from the Patriarch of Constantinople. Indeed Balkan nationalism seemed to be directed as much against

Greek cultural and religious domination as against Turkish political rule. Serbia attained political autonomy between 1812 and 1829 and independence in 1878; in a parallel development, the Archbishop of Belgrade was recognized as Metropolitan of Serbia in 1832 and the independence of the Serbian Church was conceded in 1878.[3] The Rumanian principalities were placed under native instead of Phanariot princes in the 1820's and acquired first autonomy, then union, and finally independence; Greek domination of the Church was ended in 1861 and its independence from the Patriarchate was acknowledged in 1873. The Bulgarians, long the most oppressed by both Turks and Phanariots, were made a separate *millet* in 1870 and declared their ecclesiastical independence under an elected Exarch in 1872. The Patriarch refused to recognize the new Exarchate and excommunicated its adherents, a situation which persisted even after Bulgaria became independent in 1878; but the Bulgarian Church was accepted by other Orthodox bodies. The loss by Turkey of its remaining Balkan territories in the twentieth century resulted in the jurisdiction of the Patriarch being confined to the Orthodox of Turkey proper, virtually all of whom lived in Constantinople.

Eastern Orthodoxy came to be divided into national churches, each dependent on its own nation-state, yet maintaining communion with each other and acknowledging the nominal primacy of the Oecumenical Patriarch. The overthrow of the Turks was accompanied by the overthrow of the Phanariots, a blessing for the churches that was obtained at the price of disunity. In no other segment of Christianity has the fate of the churches been so intimately bound up with the rise and victory of nationalism.

Alone among Orthodox nations, Russia had preserved its independence and had emerged as one of the great powers of Europe. With the fall of Constantinople to the Turks in 1453, the mantle of Byzantium had fallen upon the ruler of Moscow, the "third Rome," the final seat both of empire and of the Church. Since the Patriarch of Constantinople was a Turkish puppet,

[3] After the South Slavs were united under the Jugoslav state, the historic Patriarchate of Peč was revived in 1920.

Moscow declared itself an independent Patriarchate, and the Russian Church became the most important segment of Eastern Orthodoxy.

The Russian Orthodox Church never experienced a shock comparable to the Reformation, but its course was significantly altered by two traumatic events in the late seventeenth and early eighteenth centuries. The first developed from a movement of liturgical reform led by the Patriarch Nikon after 1652, which was resisted vigorously, if ignorantly, by traditionalist elements in the Church supported by a large part of the peasantry. The result was a schism of the "Old Believers," perhaps one-sixth of the population, who split into a variety of sects which often tended to reject the state as well as the Church, producing a strain of messianic radicalism which runs through subsequent Russian history. The second traumatic event was the drastic Westernization of the state and the higher elements of society by Peter the Great and his successors in the eighteenth century. Since the Church, an essentially conservative force, resisted Westernization, Peter deprived it of its independence, abolished the Patriarchate, and replaced it with a Holy Synod directed by a lay Procurator. These reforms, however, touched only the surface of Russian life. The great mass of the Russian people were peasants in a state of degrading serfdom, who remained devotedly attached to the old ways. The result was a profound division in Russian life: the dominant social and intellectual elements adopted Western ways and views, while the bulk of the people were still semi-Asiatic in their habits and outlook.

The nineteenth century produced no events in Russian church history of comparable drama or significance. Rather, it saw the maturation of the devotional genius of Russian Orthodoxy and the working-out of the consequences of subordinating the Church to the imperial government. By the end of the eighteenth century, the Church had lost its independence but not its wealth. The monasteries, from whom the bishops were drawn, played an especially important role, while the parish priests, almost an hereditary caste, were ill-educated, poorly paid, and virtually indistinguishable from the peasants whom they served. The in-

tellectual elements of society were attracted to the secular interests of Western Europe, and the Church produced few theologians of importance. It expended its energies instead on worship,
with its rich liturgy and impressive iconography, and on private
devotion.

The nineteenth century witnessed a revival of the spirituality
of Russian Orthodoxy, inspired by one of the most distinctive
features of Russian devotional life, the *startsi* (elders). The
startsi were intense ascetics, usually monks, who were much
sought after as spiritual counsellors; their influence produced
something parallel to the evangelical awakening in Western
Europe. A notable center of the *startsi* was the monastery of
Optina Pustyn. The most famous nineteenth-century *starets* was
St. Serafim of Sarov, who popularized the devotional repetition
of the "Jesus prayer": "O Lord Jesus Christ, thou Son of God, be
merciful to me, a sinner." The awakening was reinforced by a
revival of patristic studies, particularly the study of the devotional writings of the Greek Fathers; a collection of patristic
excerpts on the life of the spirit, the *Philokalia,* was translated
into Russian and was widely read.

The most important intellectual contributions of nineteenth-
century Russian Orthodoxy were made not by clergymen but by
laymen. While the dominant tendencies of lay thought were
Westernized and secular, there was a movement of reaction
against Western influence which emphasized the distinctive
character of the Russian people, especially the peasantry, and
hence stressed the virtues of the Orthodox religion. This exalta-
tion of the Slavic element, highly idealized, is called Slavophil-
ism. The most eminent philosopher of the Slavophiles was A. S.
Khomiakov, who argued that salvation comes through the
sobornost, the church community considered as an organic whole.
The Orthodox Church was the purest expression of Christian
brotherhood, while Western churches, Roman Catholic or Protestant, were too individualistic. The ideal of Orthodox brotherhood was found in the peasants, whose passive spirituality, with
its emphasis on redemption through suffering, was described in
the novels of Dostoevsky. Dostoevsky had begun his career as a

Westernized, radical intellectual but experienced a religious conversion while exiled in Siberia. Another who turned from Western secularism to Orthodoxy was V. S. Soloviev, a mystical philosopher who devoted himself to the reunion of the Churches. In the early twentieth century, partly under Soloviev's influence, there began a renaissance of Orthodox religious philosophy which bore belated fruit in the works of the ex-Marxists Berdyaev and Bulgakov.

Probably the greatest religious writer of nineteenth-century Russia was Leo Tolstoy, whose development followed the familiar course of a Westernized education followed by a return to the simple virtues of the Russian peasants. In Tolstoy's case, however, this religious conversion was accompanied by a revulsion against the actual Orthodox Church. He developed his own creed, founded on the words "resist not evil," which enjoined compassion for all living creatures, brotherhood in a propertyless community, and abstention from war and state service. Tolstoy was excommunicated by the Church he had abandoned. Although he formed no cult of his own, his works had considerable influence.

The ideal which Tolstoy preached might be found among some of those peasants who had left the Church and joined various sects of Old Believers. Scattered and often persecuted, the Old Believers or *raskolniki* (rebels) tended to divide and to produce new sects, some of them rather exotic. The more conservative *popovtsi* accepted the services of priests ordained by the established Church, and some of them returned eventually to its communion. The more radical groups had no priests and were highly fragmented. Among the older groups were the Khlysty, who believed in contemporary incarnations of Christ, and their offshoots, the Skoptsy, who often castrated themselves, and the communistic Dukhobors ("spirit-wrestlers"), who suffered persecution for their refusal of military service and emigrated to Canada in 1898–1899. From the Dukhobors arose the Molokans ("Milk-drinkers") who held that the Bible was the sole authority for faith. In the nineteenth century, under Protestant influences, Stundist and other Baptist groups were formed.

All deviation from the Orthodox Church was opposed, sometimes with severe persecution, by the state. In the nineteenth century, the Tsar, "Autocrat of all the Russias," was the bulwark of reaction in Europe. Both to unify the empire and to resist the liberal and radical influences of Western Europe, the Russian Orthodox Church was exalted and utilized by the state. Minority groups—Old Believers, Uniate Catholics,[4] and Jews—were persecuted in the attempt to force them to accept Orthodoxy. A repressive censorship sought to prevent the introduction of liberal ideas from the West, and Siberia was turned into a prison-camp for radical intellectuals. Under Tsar Nicholas I (1825–1855), the alliance of reaction and religion was well-nigh complete, and even the moderately reforming Metropolitan Philaret of Moscow was restricted in his activities. Under the next Tsar, Alexander II, who liberated the serfs, there was a period of relative liberalism, but the succeeding reigns brought a return of reaction.

The ablest exponent of Orthodox reaction, and indeed one of the most noteworthy religious laymen of the century, was K. P. Pobiedonostsev, a lawyer who became Procurator of the Holy Synod in 1880 and intellectually dominated Tsars Alexander III and Nicholas II. Pobiedonostsev regarded the Russian Orthodox Church as the true embodiment of the faith of the people and the last bulwark of Christianity against the disintegrating forces of Western liberalism. The Church was to be closely allied with the state and should unite, under the autocratic rule of the Tsar, the various peoples of his empire. Pobiedonostsev fostered parochial schools, improved the education of the priests, and promoted Orthodox missions to the non-Christian peoples of Asiatic Russia. Less constructively, he used his power to repress all opposition and promoted a policy of "Russification" of minority nationalities. When a revolution came in 1905, he was removed from office.

[4] Large numbers of Ukrainians (Ruthenians), formerly under Polish rule, had submitted to Rome while retaining their own rite. After the partitions of Poland they came under Russian rule and efforts were made to bring them back to the Orthodox fold. Several millions returned to Orthodoxy by 1839; those who remained loyal to Rome were often persecuted.

Despite the revival of Orthodox faith and thought and the repressive activities of the state, the dominant tendencies among the intellectual class were those of Western secularism, growing more radical throughout the century. The "intelligentsia"—a hybrid class whose half-Latin, half-Russian name betrays its origins—found themselves alienated from the existing society and the state and Church which sought to preserve it unchanged. Even the seminaries, in which the sons of the clergy were educated to follow their fathers' profession, produced a majority of unbelievers. Except for a minority of Slavophiles, the intellectuals were both politically revolutionary and hostile to religion. Late in the century Marxism began to appeal to them. While the Marxists could draw no following from the peasants, the beginnings of industrialism in Russia produced a proletariat in the larger towns which was potentially revolutionary.

A widespread revolution in 1905 proved premature, although it produced a partial reversal of the policy of Pobiedonostsev, including the end of the persecution of the Old Believers and of the efforts to Russify the minorities. The reforms after 1905 were insufficient to meet either the discontent or the needs of the Russian people, and the best efforts of reformers were nullified by the weakness of Tsar Nicholas II and the sinister influence of the mad monk Rasputin. When the defeat of Russia in World War I brought about revolution in 1917, the monarchy collapsed. The momentary hope that the Russian Orthodox Church might improve its situation now that it was free from the dominance of the crown was crushed when a second stage of the revolution brought to power the Bolsheviks, the left wing of the Marxists. Henceforth the Church was to suffer a persecution more severe than it had imposed on its opponents. The close association of Church and state, a characteristic feature of Orthodoxy but peculiarly marked in Russia, left the Church defenseless when catastrophe overtook the state on which it had relied.

16

Ecumenical Movements

A narrative history of nineteenth-century Christianity tends inevitably to emphasize the differences and discords among the various churches and movements. Such an emphasis is not entirely unwarranted: the churches tended to turn inward upon themselves, devoting a large part of their attention to internal doctrine and discipline at a time when the external challenges to the Christian religion were rising. There was much to be said, in an age full of dangerous novelties, for maintaining the integrity of the faith and the order of the church; but such emphases tended to harden the divisions of Christendom. In the twentieth century, the realization of the difficulties caused by these divisions has brought about the rise of the Ecumenical Movement.[1] So characteristic of this century is ecumenism that its nineteenth-century origins have been almost forgotten, and it is conventional to speak of the movement as having begun with the Edinburgh Conference of 1910. Yet the nineteenth century, though far less congenial to ecumenism, witnessed a series of ecumenical movements, some of them abortive and some destined to pave the way for the larger movements of the present day.

[1] The word "ecumenical" (from the Greek *oikumene*, the whole inhabited world) has historically signified the actions of the Church as a whole, as in "ecumenical councils." The modern usage of "ecumenical" relates to a) efforts at cooperation or merger of several denominations, and b) the spirit of fellowship and aspiration for the unity of all Christians. The branch of theology pertaining to this subject is called "ecumenics," a term which seems to have superseded the older "eirenics."

Most of the movements which have borne fruit in the twentieth century derived from the evangelical Protestant tradition, but several of the most interesting and ambitious schemes of church union had non-evangelical sources. The most obvious instance of this was the union of the Lutheran and Reformed *Landeskirchen* in Germany at the command of the absolutist princes. The dangers inherent in such enforced unions were made clear by the sharp reaction of the confessional Lutherans, which illustrates what may be called the first law of ecumenics: for every union there is a secession, weaker in numbers but stronger in doctrine. Nonetheless the Evangelical Church of Prussia was the largest Protestant church in Europe; and from the same monarchical leadership came an even more ambitious project of interchurch cooperation. The romantic Frederick William IV, influenced by his minister Bunsen and attracted by the episcopal system of church government, sought a *rapprochement* with the Church of England by founding, in 1841, a joint Anglo-Prussian bishopric in Jerusalem. The project met much opposition, especially from the High Anglicans, on the ground that it represented merely administrative rather than doctrinal unity. It was abandoned in 1886.

Another source of ecumenical projects was the Anglo-Catholic movement in the Church of England. The *via media* adopted by the Anglo-Catholics made them extremely conscious of the major divisions of Christianity and their relationship to the "one holy catholic Church" in which all believed. Some Anglo-Catholics adopted the "branch" theory of the Church—the idea that the three episcopally-governed communions, Anglican, Roman Catholic, and Eastern Orthodox—were equally valid branches of the universal Church. The outcome of this theory was the idea of corporate reunion, a project to reunite the Church by a merger of the three branches acting as units. To this end the Association for the Promotion of Christian Unity was founded in 1857 by some High Churchmen and sympathetic Roman Catholics; but it was condemned by Rome in 1864 on the ground that the hope of corporate reunion merely served to delay individual conversions to Roman Catholicism. The movement was continued by a few

Anglo-Catholic ministers in the form of the secret Order of Corporate Reunion, led by F. G. Lee, Vicar of Lambeth. The great difficulty for the corporate reunionists was the question of the validity of Anglican orders, which Rome did not accept; and when Leo XIII formally declared Anglican orders invalid in 1896, the movement came to an end. For many of its members it had been only a way-station on the road to conversion.

The only significantly favorable Roman Catholic response to this tendency in Anglo-Catholicism came from Döllinger, who kept throughout his career the hope of the reunion of the Churches. He sought to further this project by personal contacts with leading Lutherans and High Anglicans and by his historical work, designed to promote unity by removing unfounded prejudices. Even after his excommunication in 1871 he continued in this course, and the Old Catholic Church organized by his disciples [2] regarded itself as a bridge between Anglicanism and Orthodoxy. Under Döllinger's presidency conferences were held at Bonn in 1874 and 1875, attended by Anglicans, Old Catholics, and Orthodox. Although these meetings produced no immediate results, contacts between Anglican and Orthodox leaders were maintained and eventually resulted in the mutual recognition of each other's orders.

These were the most ambitious ecumenical endeavors of the nineteenth century. With the Roman Catholic Church in a "state of siege," insisting that unity could come only by submission to Rome, there was a limit to the success which such endeavors could then achieve. The more successful ecumenical movements were those which confined themselves to Protestant denominations; indeed, until very recently, the word "ecumenical" has had the practical meaning of pan-Protestant. These movements were the product of the evangelical tradition.[3] In

[2] Döllinger himself declined to join the Old Catholic Church because of its schismatic character.

[3] An exception to this rule was the "Mercersburg theology" of Philip Schaff and John W. Nevin, who criticized American revivalistic evangelicalism and sought Christian unity in the historic church and its sacraments, understood in Calvin's sense. Schaff's historical works were useful prolegomena to the ecumenical movement.

England and the United States, the countries most affected by the evangelical revival, patterns of alliance among Protestant denominations were most fully developed, and from these countries came the inspiration for international organizations of Protestant cooperation.

One of the first of these movements was the Evangelical Alliance, founded in England in 1846. It was an association of individuals rather than of churches, and from the first it enrolled members from other nations, especially America, where a branch was founded in 1867. Emphasizing religious liberty and hostility towards the Roman Catholic Church,[4] the Evangelical Alliance held frequent international meetings.

More important in engendering habits of inter-denominational cooperation was the work of the Young Men's Christian Associations. The first YMCA was founded in London in 1844; American YMCA's were started in 1852; and in 1855 a World Alliance of YMCA's was formed. The YMCA was expressly undenominational, with an evangelical bias and lay leadership; its emphasis gradually shifted from evangelism to social activity.[5] The American YMCA organized a Student Division to work on college campuses, and from this developed the World Student Christian Federation, founded by John R. Mott in 1895. Mott also organized the Student Volunteer Movement for Foreign Missions, founded in 1886 with the motto "the evangelization of the world in our generation." Another youth movement, influential at the end of the century, was Christian Endeavor. The student Christian movements supplied much of the leadership and inspiration for the ecumenism of the twentieth century.

Another source of ecumenism was the organization, in countries with several Protestant churches, of national inter-church organizations. The German *Landeskirchen* sent representatives to annual *Kirchentagen* and conferences after 1848, which pro-

---

[4] A precursor of the Evangelical Alliance was the Protestant Alliance, founded in the 1830's on a specifically anti-Catholic platform.

[5] The Young Women's Christian Associations followed a parallel course. Another international organization under lay leadership was the World Sunday School Convention, founded in 1889, which prepared a uniform Sunday School curriculum.

moted the uniform development of the various churches. The Inner Mission was organized on a national basis. The cantonal churches of Switzerland formed a national conference in 1858, and the various Protestant churches of France formed a federation in 1905. In England the division between the Establishment and Nonconformity prevented full cooperation among Protestant bodies, but organizations such as the Evangelical Alliance and the Bible and tract societies brought together both Anglican and Dissenting evangelicals. The older Nonconformist groups had long been in the habit of working together for political objects, and a National Free Church Council was formally organized in 1892.

The country most prominent in the formation of interdenominational Protestant organizations was the United States of America. Such a development was natural in view of the proliferation of denominations and the fact that most of these shared a common evangelical base. The characteristic pattern of interdenominational activity was the voluntary society for evangelism or philanthropy, such as the American Board of Commissioners for Foreign Missions, the American Sunday School Union, the American Bible Society, and organizations for home missions and temperance. The "benevolent empire" of these organizations embraced individuals rather than churches, although the Congregationalists and Presbyterians agreed to a Plan of Union in 1801 for missions to the settlers in the West. Rising denominationalism halted the growth of the societies after the 1830's, but it was resumed in the last third of the century, aided by the vogue of the "social gospel." Largely to coordinate the social service activities of the denominations, the Federal Council of Churches was formed in 1908, the forerunner of the present National Council of Churches.

While these associations cut across denominational lines, the various denominational groups developed their own patterns of international organization. The most striking of these was the development of Anglicanism from a national church to an international communion. The established Church of England, disestablished in America and in the British colonies, produced independent churches in each country, united only by historical and sentimental connections and by the episcopal form of government. Beginning in 1888, the bishops of the Anglican communion met decenially in the Lambeth Conferences, developing a bond of fellowship rather than a synodical organization and giving a new sense of common purpose to Anglicanism.[6] Similarly, an international alliance of Reformed and Presbyterian churches was formed in 1875, and international councils of Methodists, Congregationalists, and Baptists were organized in 1881, 1891, and 1905, respectively. The habit of international cooperation, even within denominational limits, was a necessary preliminary to subsequent ecumenical developments.

The most important source of ecumenism was the missionary movement. In no other endeavor did Protestant denominations have so long an experience of cooperation. In the mission field, it was quickly discovered that the divisions among Christians were both irrelevant and harmful, deterring converts by making Christianity appear self-contradictory. The movement towards union has consequently been more vigorously pressed by the "Younger Churches" than by their European sponsors. The necessity of coordinating missionary activities was also recognized by the countries sending out missionaries, and from the 1850's there was a series of conferences on missions. The American and British evangelicals, who supplied the majority of Protestant missionaries, took the leading role in these conferences. Meanwhile national organizations of missionary cooperation were formed in the last decades of the century.

The climax of this development was the Edinburgh World Missionary Conference of 1910, which marks a milestone in the history of the ecumenical movement. Unlike previous conferences, the Edinburgh meeting emphasized careful study and planning, organized by John Mott, and it brought together not

6 The Conference of 1888 adopted a proposal for Protestant unity advanced by an American Episcopalian, William R. Huntington. The "Lambeth Quadrilateral" was based on four essential principles: the Scriptures as the rule of faith, the Apostles' and Nicene Creeds as the sufficient statement of faith, the two sacraments of Baptism and the Lord's Supper, and the historic episcopate. The last item was unacceptable to non-Anglicans.

merely interested individuals but official representatives of the churches. Moreover, the Anglo-American evangelical emphasis was complemented by the presence of native spokesmen of the "Younger Churches" and also by the inclusion of continental Lutherans and of High Anglicans, making this conference more truly ecumenical in both the geographical and the doctrinal sense. Questions of faith and order were excluded from the discussions, but the fruitful confrontation of representatives of different points of view made it evident that there were wider possibilities of interchurch discussion than had been realized. Most important, the conference set up a continuation committee, which provided for further meetings and studies and ultimately developed into the International Missionary Council, founded in 1921.

World War I provided only a brief interruption in the series of international conferences for which Edinburgh 1910 had set the example. The ecumenical movement inspired by the missionary conferences was carried forward by other groups: the "Life and Work" movement of social ethics led by Nathan Söderblom, Archbishop of Uppsala, and the "Faith and Order" discussions largely sponsored by the Anglo-Catholics. From these origins came the World Council of Churches, founded in 1948, in which most major Protestant and Orthodox denominations joined.

It would be premature to assess the significance of these ecumenical tendencies. The basic theological tensions have not been resolved; indeed, the rise of ecumenism and "dialogue" has coincided with the revival of orthodoxy and doctrinal emphases. The ecumenical movement, for nearly half a century, did not include Roman Catholics, and several of the conservative Protestant denominations held aloof. Nonetheless, the degree of cooperation attained by the international conferences and organizations represents the largest measure of unity Christianity has known since the Reformation. The ecumenical movement may prove to be, as some have called it, the most important religious development of the twentieth century. To this development, the nineteenth century made significant if tentative contributions.

17

Expansions of Europe

This narrative has thus far been concerned primarily with events in Europe, which remained, throughout the nineteenth century, the heartland of Christendom. At the same time, however, a "larger Europe" was emerging in the areas of European settlement overseas, particularly the Americas and Australasia. By the end of the century, some of these newer nations were ready to take their part in the leadership of the Christian world. This was especially true of the United States of America, whose rich religious development must receive separate treatment. Two other areas also deserve notice. The first is that part of the British Empire which consisted of settlement colonies: Canada, Australia, New Zealand, and (to an extent) South Africa. The second is Latin America, which had been conquered and partially Europeanized by Spaniards and Portuguese in the sixteenth century. In both areas Christianity was the hereditary faith of the European population; the problem was to preserve their faith in the new environment.

The religious history of the "larger Europe" is at once an extension of the European story and a part of the story of the Christian missions to the non-European world. Indeed, much of the "missionary" effort of the age was devoted to providing the services of religion to the emigrants from Europe. Further, the religious history of these new nations is only a part of the larger story of the Atlantic Migration, the greatest movement of people ever known. Some fifty million Europeans left Europe in the course of a century. This was the largest geographical expansion in the history of European civilization, and, incidentally, of Christianity. Its significance, however, did not become fully evident until the collapse of the old Europe after 1914.

Canada, the most important of the British settlement colonies after the American Revolution, provided the model for colonial development through several stages of self-government to the attainment of "Dominion" status in 1867. There was one element, however, which rendered Canada atypical: the presence of a large population of French origin, established prior to the British conquest in 1759, which retained its distinct nationality and its attachment to the Roman Catholic religion. After 1783 there was an influx of American "loyalists" who were continually reinforced by emigrants from the British Isles throughout the nineteenth century. These new arrivals, with the exception of the Irish, brought with them the varieties of British Protestantism to which they were accustomed. The result was that Canada had, in effect, two religious histories, one Catholic and one Protestant.

The history of the Roman Catholic Church in Canada is intimately bound up with that of the French nationality, which ultimately represented one-quarter of the total population and a large majority in the province of Québec. In a rare act of statesmanship, the British government, anti-Catholic at home, allowed the Roman Catholic Church to retain its traditional privileges in Canada, including the right to collect tithes from its members. The Church remained a dominant force in the history of the province of Québec. In the other provinces the Catholics were in a minority, and the leadership of the French was contested by a large Irish element. In non-French Canada, unassisted by the government, Roman Catholicism experienced a development similar to that in the United States. By the end of the century a full ecclesiastical structure had been developed in both French and non-French Canada.

The Protestantism of Canada was overwhelmingly of British origin, with Anglicans, Presbyterians, and Methodists providing the largest elements. Most of the Protestant immigration came during and after the period of the evangelical revival, which contributed to the success of the churches in holding the majority of the immigrants to the faith. Missionary societies in the British Isles were responsible for providing most of the early ministers and teachers, but by the latter part of the century the Canadian churches had established numerous colleges and universities of their own. The Anglicans developed a full hierarchy, the first bishop being consecrated in 1787 and an archbishopric erected in 1860. The development of the Presbyterian Church was hampered for some time by divisions which paralleled those of Scotland, but union was achieved in 1875. The Methodists enjoyed the most rapid expansion, becoming for a while the largest single denomination.

Canadian Protestantism had to deal with two major church-state controversies. The Anglicans and Presbyterians, representing the established churches of Britain, sought a similar establishment in Canada; and an act of 1791, which separated Upper Canada (Ontario) from Québec, provided lands for the maintenance of a "Protestant clergy." This caused a half-century of strife among the various churches until the "clergy reserves" were transferred to governmental use in 1854. This marked the effective separation of church and state. Another controversy arose, as usual in the nineteenth century, over the schools. In 1841 separate publicly-supported school systems were established for Protestants and Roman Catholics. Gradually, however, most of the provinces, except Québec, withdrew public funds from denominational schools, and most public education in Canada became secular. This does not appear to have been harmful to the churches. By contrast with the United States, the vast majority of the population retained church affiliations.

Australia was settled almost exclusively from the British Isles. The first settlers were convicts, and the first clergymen were chaplains to the penal colonies. Free settlers eventually came to be the majority of the immigrants, especially after the discovery of gold in the 1850's. The chief problem for the churches, aside from the undesirable character of many of the immigrants, was that of space: the several colonies were remote from each other and from the mother country, which for a long time supplied most of the clergy, and much of the population was thinly scattered in rural areas. Australia was slower in attaining maturity than Canada: Dominion status was achieved in 1900. However, by the end of the century, viable local churches had been developed. The largest church was the Anglican, with some forty per cent of the population; Presbyterians and Methodists were the two other substantial Protestant groups. Roman Catholics numbered only twenty per cent, nearly all of them Irish. As in Canada, the chief issues were establishment and education. For some decades a system of plural establishment was maintained, with subsidies given to the Anglican, Presbyterian, Methodist, and Roman Catholic churches; but this was abandoned by 1871. Similarly, after an experiment with denominational schools, public education came to be secular.

In New Zealand, British settlement had been preceded by missions to the Polynesian (Maori) natives. The first British emigrants, beginning in 1840, came in planned denominational colonies—Christchurch settled by Anglicans and Otago by Presbyterians—and these two groups became the largest Protestant churches. Settlement was retarded by wars with the Maoris, who eventually were able to become an integral part of the nation, most of them professing Christianity. The development of the churches paralleled that of Australia.

South Africa was a special case among settlement colonies, since the European immigrants and their descendants shared the area with a larger African (Bantu) population. The two races remained separate, and the history of Christianity among the Bantu is part of the story of the missions rather than the settlements. The original settlers were Dutch (Boers), adherents of the Reformed Church. After the Cape of Good Hope was transferred to British rule at the beginning of the nineteenth century, many of the Boers trekked inland to form autonomous republics, the Transvaal and the Orange Free State, which were only reduced to submission in 1902. Thus the Boers remained a nationality apart, adhering to a conservative pietistic form of Calvinism.

British settlement came after 1815, with the Anglicans [1] and Methodists being the largest denominations; the Roman Catholic element was smaller than usual. The problems of religion in South Africa tended to be subsumed in the larger problem of relations between the British and Boer nationalities and between the white and black races.

In general,[2] the settlement areas of the British empire witnessed a relatively successful transplantation of the leading forms of British Christianity. Within less than a century, the local churches were self-sufficient and often ready to undertake missionary work of their own. They largely succeeded in retaining the allegiance of the European settlers, even though state support of the churches was soon terminated. They made no original contributions to religion, but they demonstrated that Christianity was capable of satisfactory adjustment to new surroundings.

Prior to the nineteenth century, the most extensive transplantation of Christianity and European civilization had been in Latin America. After the conquests of the early sixteenth century, Spain and Portugal had built up colonial empires in which, although pure-blooded Europeans were in the minority, the essential institutions of European culture and religion had been established. Except for the Indians of the unexplored interior, the entire population adhered to the Roman Catholic Church, which developed a full hierarchy. In the nineteenth century, however, Latin America was the region in which Christianity was least successful. The contrast with the other expansions of Christianity in this century revealed the superficiality of the Christian

[1] The progress of Anglicanism in South Africa was somewhat hindered by the controversy over Bishop Colenso.

[2] A special case is that of the British West Indies, where European settlement was accompanied by a larger population of Negroes, slaves until 1834. The Church of England was established until 1870. The various denominations engaged in missionary work among the Negroes, most of whom became nominal Christians, although it is questionable to what extent they were actually affected by the Christian religion. Most of the problems were the aftermath of slavery.

impact on Latin America and the unfortunate heritage of Spanish and Portuguese conquest and rule.

The Roman Catholic Church which Spain and Portugal imposed on their American colonies was entirely dependent upon the state. The kings held the *real patronato*—full powers of appointment of all clergymen, from archbishops to parish priests— and exercised minute control over the actions of the Church which, although endowed with great wealth, was an enervated and passive institution. The colonies never produced enough clergy for their needs, and many of the priests sent from Europe were of low quality.[3] The Church was caught in the conflicts of the native whites (*creoles*), the mixed bloods (*mestizos*), and the Spaniards. These problems came to a head when, during the embroilment of Spain in the Napoleonic wars, her colonies (except Cuba and Puerto Rico) began to revolt from her rule. Despite Spanish efforts at reconquest, her colonial empire had by 1830 been transformed into a dozen independent republics. Meanwhile Brazil had, with less conflict, established her independence from Portugal.

The independence of the Spanish American states was a shock to the Church. Most of the higher clergy had supported the Spanish regime against the rebels, and Spain maintained its claims to ecclesiastical control even after political power had been lost. The Papacy, committed to the Spanish government and the principle of monarchical legitimacy, refused for many years to recognize the new republics, which, in turn, made their own claims to ecclesiastical patronage and would not admit bishops appointed by Spain. At one time thirty out of thirty-eight sees were vacant. The impasse was only resolved in the 1830's; but meanwhile Spanish-American Catholicism had experienced a severe dislocation, and the number of clergy had declined significantly.

The political instability of the new republics was another difficulty for the Church. Power oscillated between conservatives and liberals, or rather between the military leaders of the factions.

[3] Notable exceptions were the religious orders, particularly the Jesuits and Franciscans, who worked effectively among the Indians. The expulsion of the Jesuits in 1769 was disastrous for the missions.

The conservatives tended to support the Church, often to the extent of forbidding all non-Catholic worship. The liberals, on the other hand, were anti-clerical; influenced by the Enlightenment and later by Positivism,[4] they sought to disestablish the Church, reduce its great wealth, and restrict the religious orders. The alternation in power of these factions produced extremes of clericalism and of persecution which were unsettling to both the political and the religious life of the region.

The most dramatic illustration of this situation was the case of Mexico. Here the Church, established as the state religion by the first Constitution, was said to own one-quarter of the land. Liberal governments in the 1830's attempted to nationalize the property of the religious orders and to exercise the power of ecclesiastical patronage. A conservative reaction under the dictator Santa Anna undid their work. When he was expelled in 1855, the liberals sought to nationalize all the property of the Church and otherwise restrict its power. When it appeared that the great liberal leader Benito Juarez would completely separate the state from the Church, the conservatives called for foreign intervention, and France set up a short-lived puppet empire. The final triumph of Juarez in 1867 resulted in the separation of Church and state, the liquidation of the Church lands, and other restrictions on the Church. Under the long dictatorship of Diaz (1876-1911), the restrictions on the Church were relaxed and a *modus vivendi* was attained. The revolution of 1911 was not initially anti-Catholic; but Catholic support for a conservative counter-revolution in 1913, which ultimately failed, brought about the most severe persecution of the Church in modern times. For nearly two decades the operations of the Church were virtually suspended, most of the clergy being slain or exiled. Not until the late 1930's was some normalization of relations achieved.

The case of Mexico, though far from unique, was extreme. In Brazil, independence brought about no dislocation; and even

[4] Another anti-clerical philosophy was Krausism, a modification of pantheism devised by an otherwise obscure German, K. C. F. Krause, which was influential in Spain and Spanish America.

when Church and state were separated in 1890, there was little conflict. The Church remained established in several nations, particularly along the west coast of South America,[5] where conservative governments were in power most of the time. In other countries, however, the Church was disestablished.

Certain problems were common to all countries.[6] Latin America never produced enough priests for its needs, and the quality of the priesthood was low. The small but important intellectual class was consistently secularist in its outlook. The growing urban proletariat was largely unreached by the Church. While the vast majority of the population professed Roman Catholicism, their religion was passive and often merely nominal. So great was the religious void that an opportunity seemed to be open for Protestant missions. An extensive missionary effort was undertaken which, however, did not reach fruition until the twentieth century, especially after the arrival of the Pentecostal sects. Protestant missionaries were most successful with the jungle Indians and with elements of the urban masses, but the largest Protestant groups in South America were the results of an extensive European immigration, particularly in Argentina, Brazil, and Chile. Indeed Europe supplied most of the vigor of Roman Catholicism as well as of Protestantism in the region. The heritage of the conquest and of the colonial era had been the enervation of Latin-American Christianity, which had proved inadequate to meet the challenges of the nineteenth-century revolutions.

[5] One conservative president of Ecuador dedicated the entire country to the Sacred Heart.

[6] We may include in this survey the Philippine Islands, ruled by Spain until 1898. Here, as in Latin America, most of the population were nominal Catholics. Resentment against the Spanish clergy and the wealthy religious orders led, at the end of the century, to the Aglipayan schism; several hundred thousand people joined the new Filipino Independent Church. The transfer to American rule brought an influx of Protestant missionaries, but it also stimulated a Roman Catholic revival, made possible by the importation of new priests from America and Europe. The lands of the religious orders were disposed of by a settlement negotiated by William Howard Taft.

The transplantation of the Christian faith to the settlement colonies of the British Empire represents one of the victories of nineteenth-century Christianity; the weakening of Christianity in Latin America was perhaps its greatest defeat. The contrast cannot be explained by the fact that the British Empire was largely Protestant while Latin America was Roman Catholic, for the British Catholics shared in the religious vitality of their Empire. It may perhaps be explained by cultural factors—the peculiar narrowness of Iberian Catholicism and the problems of a mixed (Spanish, Indian, and Negro) population. The political situation may have had a significant effect; the British colonies developed in relative freedom, with a fairly early and easy separation of Church and state, while Latin America had the heritage of the Inquisition and the *real patronato,* and the position of a Church so intimately related to the state became a bone of contention between political factions. Yet it may be unnecessary to seek special causes to explain the contrast. Throughout the nineteenth century, and perhaps in other eras, Christianity was most successful where it was newest, where it came relatively fresh, as in the largely virgin areas of the British Empire and the United States. It was least successful where it had been long and easily established, and particularly in an area such as Latin America, where the superficiality of its penetration was cruelly revealed in the revolutionary turmoil which accompanied the winning of political independence.

18

America: Land of Experiment

The history of religion in the United States of America is one of the great success stories of the nineteenth century. In Europe, the pattern of religious history had been revival followed by crisis; in America, the pattern was revival followed by consolidation. The elements of religious revival with which the century opened worked their way in America relatively unchecked by the counter-tendencies which limited their effect in Europe. They have left a permanent impress on the character of the American nation, which is at once the child of Europe and a new creation.

American religious history has had such a unique character, demonstrated such a distinct creativity, and developed so extensive a literature, that it cannot adequately be treated as a chapter in the religious history of Europe.[1] In a volume such as this, a chapter on America can be but a brief note, pointing out those things which have made the American religious experience significantly different from the European. At the same time, it must be realized that the American experience took its point of departure from the European and was affected by European developments before and during the nineteenth century. Students of American religion must understand European history in order to appreciate both American origins and American uniqueness. Historians of European religion will find the American experience most

[1] It is hoped that another book in this series will be devoted exclusively to American religious history.

199

instructive precisely in its deviations from the European pattern, which strikingly illustrate the potentialities of the nineteenth-century revival of religion.

The first thing which confronts the European observer of America is the sheer size of the country. Simply to have carried the customs and institutions of religion across the ocean and then across the continent would have been a major achievement. What makes the American experience distinctive is the fact that European Christianity was not simply reproduced, as in the British colonies, but modified. Alone among the "new nations," America displayed real creativity in religion.

At the time of independence, less than ten per cent of the population, nearly all of whom were of Protestant origin, were members of any church. Some historians even speak of revolutionary America as a "de-Christianized" country with a "heathen" population. This interpretation is belied by the readiness of response which greeted the great revivals only a generation after independence. There must have been a good deal of latent Christianity in these unchurched people. Membership statistics always understate the degree of religious adherence among Americans.[2] In Europe, a man may be a church member without believing in God; in America, a man may be deeply religious without being a member of any church. Nonetheless, the rise of church membership indicates the trend of conscious religious commitment. In a rapidly growing population, church membership rose to 15.5 per cent in 1850, 35.7 per cent in 1900, 43.5 in 1910, and well over sixty per cent at the present time. Whatever the value of these statistics, they indicate that the trend was upwards—the reverse of what was happening in Europe.

This growth was accomplished almost entirely by voluntary action, without the assistance of the state. The ideal of "a free

2 Religious statistics are never very reliable. Each denomination has its own definition of membership, and most American Protestant bodies count only enrolled or active members, excluding children and informal adherents. Thus the membership figures are much smaller than the actual influence of the Protestant denominations.

Church in a free state," which Europe was unable to attain, was realized in the United States. The separation of Church and state was made possible by two factors. First, the factor of space played in the new nation of America the role which time had played in Europe.[3] Until the end of the nineteenth century there was always empty space beyond the settled areas, allowing to the dissatisfied the possibility of unconfined movement and preventing the hardening of rigid cultural patterns. Second, diversity in religion was already a fact among the American colonists even before independence. The American people were a mixture of nationalities, imperfectly "melted" together and repeatedly reinforced by new elements. Each group brought its distinctive faith, others were created on the new soil, and no one group was able to dominate except locally.

The brute fact of diversity made toleration inevitable and disestablishment desirable, although the chief arguments in favor of the separation of church and state were formulated by Deists such as Jefferson who used the language of universal reason: "truth is great and will prevail if left to herself." The constitution of 1787 stated that "no religious test shall ever be required as a qualification to any office or public trust under the United States." The Bill of Rights, whose provisions were later extended to the states, provided that "Congress shall make no law respecting an establishment of religion, or prohibiting the free exercise thereof." The states themselves disestablished their churches, although Massachusetts delayed until 1833. When public schools were founded in the nineteenth century, the task was too great for the limited resources of the churches and fell to the states, which developed an undenominational educational system.

The fact that public institutions were secular, however, did not mean that they were secularistic. A morality appropriate to responsible citizens, formulated in Deistic terms but based on a generalized evangelical Protestantism, was assumed and implicitly propagated. Thus the major Protestant bodies had an assured

[3] The concept of "space" is intended as an alternative formulation to that of the "frontier," which has bemused American historians since Frederick Jackson Turner.

place in American society even when separated from the state. They could not be classified in the European terms of "churches" and "sects," being neither dominant nor dissenting. The characteristic form of religious organization in America is the "denomination," a voluntary association of individuals with a common religious belief, practice, and purpose, coexisting with other denominations in a state which protects the freedom of each but favors none.

The result of this freedom was a great number and variety of denominations. The facility afforded for experiment, coupled with the American genius for organization, meant that each shade of religious opinion was able to be represented by a particular denomination. In this sense the American denomination is the counterpart of the "movement" or "school" within the more comprehensive European churches. The apparent fragmentation of American religion is not as great as might appear, although the free scope afforded to inventiveness and eccentricity has produced some extraordinary results. The majority of American denominations may be classified under a reasonably limited number of categorical headings. For this purpose it is best to employ an historical analysis.

The English settlers brought over to America both Anglicanism and various forms of nonconformity: Congregationalists, Presbyterians, Baptists, and Quakers. Significantly, the groups which were "dissenting" in England were in the majority in America. To these were added minorities of non-British origin: Dutch Reformed, German Reformed and Lutheran, Moravian and Mennonite. The first Great Awakening added the Methodists and greatly increased the Baptists; these two groups, with their offshoots, eventually comprised the majority of American Protestants. The second Awakening at the end of the eighteenth century added a number of frontier revivalist groups, notably the undoctrinal Disciples of Christ (the largest church group of purely American origin). At the same time, revivalism provoked reactions in the older churches, leading to schisms among the Presbyterians; and a counter-trend of romantic Deism formed Unitarian and Universalist churches in cultured New England.

The question of slavery was responsible for a series of schisms about mid-century, producing separate northern and southern Methodist, Baptist, and Presbyterian bodies. The freed Negroes after the Civil War formed segregated Baptist and Methodist churches of their own. Meanwhile renewed revivalism produced, as an offshoot of Methodist perfectionism, the "holiness" and later the pentecostal groups; and more eccentric by-products of revivalism included the Mormons and the millenialist sects, the Adventists and later Jehovah's Witnesses. Throughout the century immigrants were entering the country, bringing with them the faiths of continental Europe: Germans strengthened the conservative tendencies in Lutheranism, the Scandinavian nationalities formed their own Lutheran churches, and Irishmen, Germans, and later Italians and Slavs gave the Roman Catholic Church an importance it had not earlier enjoyed. The last third of the century was a period of consolidation; and the new groups that were formed, notably Christian Science, largely reflected the influence of singular personalities. By this time the pluralism of American religion was established. It should be regarded, not as fragmentation, but as the product of an historical process of repeated revivals and consolidations in which each moment of religious history was embodied in a denomination which perpetuated its unique emphasis.

The number and variety of denominations conceals a fact of equal importance: most forms of American Protestantism shared a common basis of evangelicalism. The history of religion in America, at least until the late nineteenth century, consists largely of successive revivals which formed or modified most of the Protestant denominations. The second Awakening at the close of the eighteenth century was perhaps the most significant of these revivals, but revivalism continued through the nineteenth century. The revivals were originally the product of the frontier, with its need for an unsophisticated religion with immediate emotional impact; but revivals were frequent in the cities, becoming less spontaneous but better organized under such preachers as Charles G. Finney and Dwight L. Moody. Although the theology of most preachers (except the Methodists) was more-or-less Calvinistic, the experience of conversion, with its apparently free response to God, was formulated in terms which were increasingly Arminian in their tendency. This blurring of theological lines in the interest of emotional experience did not pass without resistance, and a counter-tradition of "old Calvinism" was stronger, among formal theologians, than the free interpretation of revivalism which generally prevailed. The triumph of revivalistic evangelicalism meant that American Protestantism took on an essentially emotional rather than intellectual character; it produced little in the way of theology. It produced, instead, a "way of life." We may speak of a "core Protestantism" whose basic ingredients included the experience of conversion, reliance on the Bible, moralism, and a sense of individual responsibility.

Within this core of common feelings there developed a number of movements which transcended denominational lines. Throughout the century the evangelical impulse produced movements of social reform, notably the anti-slavery agitation and the "temperance" crusade. The sectionalism of American political life after the 1830's was reflected in the churches, with the southern groups, especially the Baptists, identifying themselves closely with the mores of their section while northern Protestantism tended to forge an alliance with the Republican party. The influence of liberal theology, largely imported from Germany, had two effects. On the one hand, there was a loosening of doctrinal standards and revivalistic emphases which allowed a rather easy accommodation to "scientific" doctrines, including those adopted by the advocates of laissez-faire economics; the older churches frequently identified themselves with the interests of their more affluent members. On the other hand, the "social gospel" represented a protest against the injustices of the age of big business. Theological liberalism tended to decline into a nearly humanistic "modernism," and the "social gospel" often manifested itself simply as humanitarian social work. In protest against this loss of distinctively Christian emphases arose a "fundamentalist" movement, strongest in rural areas, which insisted upon a return to the "fundamentals" of doctrinal Protestantism: Biblical inerrancy, the Virgin Birth, the substitutionary theory of the Atonement, the bodily resurrection and the imminent Second Coming of Jesus. The conflict between fundamentalism and liberalism was fought out within the churches rather than by the formation of new denominations. By the 1930's, however, the fundamentalist issue had come to be of less consequence than the fact that the basic postulates of "core Protestantism" were themselves being weakened by the social changes of the twentieth century.

Certain groups must be regarded as exceptions from this "core Protestantism." Some, such as the "old Calvinists," the dogmatic Lutherans, and the High Church Episcopalians, represented historic traditions which did not completely succumb to the American environment. Others, which may truly be described as "sects," were unusual variants of American religious thought which represent America's most unique contributions to Christianity. Some of these derived from the tendency to selective emphasis which is inherent in the free interpretation of the Bible. Perfectionism, which produced "holiness" and pentecostal sects, is one example of this. Dissatisfied social groups also felt the appeal of millenialism, peculiarly strong in an America which had broken with historical traditions; from this derived the Adventist bodies and later Jehovah's Witnesses. The overstimulation of repeated revivals encouraged another category of sects based upon new or supplementary revelations, such as Ann Lee's Shakers and, more significantly, Joseph Smith's Mormons.[4] Other groups based themselves upon some special knowledge or understanding, either of the Bible or of philosophy; Christian Science and Spiritualism are the leading examples of this tendency. Some of these groups go beyond the limits of identifiable Christianity. Their variety testifies to the fact that American society has liber-

---

4 Strictly speaking, Mormonism is a distinct branch of Christianity rather than a Protestant denomination, since it is based on a supplementary revelation not recognized by other Christians. The issue of polygamy has obscured a more significant feature of Mormonism, the attempt to erect a commonwealth of saints in America. This was the work largely of Brigham Young, who led the "Latter-Day Saints" to Utah, where they still retain a high degree of cohesion.

ated the prophetic impulse as well as the more conventional tendencies of religious revival.[5]

The story of Roman Catholicism in America is quite separate from the main stream of American religious history. America was a Protestant country, with a growing cultural homogeneity undergirded by an evangelical consensus. From this national consensus the Catholics were largely excluded by their authoritarian church structure, traditional doctrines, and alien origins. Most of them belonged to non-Nordic nationalities not easily assimilated into American society. The Roman Catholic Church was preeminently the Church of the immigrant. It retained a detached outlook toward American culture and was regarded as alien by most native Americans. This sense of alienation reinforced the mentality of the "state of siege" characteristic of Catholicism in Europe. Yet American Catholicism possessed some unique advantages. Although it was always regarded with suspicion and often with hostility, it was not persecuted. The openness of the American system and the constitutional guarantees of religious freedom allowed the Church full opportunity to organize and develop. We must inquire as to what use American Catholicism made of this opportunity.

At the beginning of the national history, the Catholics were an infinitesimal minority: in 1790, there were only 35,000 Catholics in a population of nearly four million. By 1900, the number of Catholics had risen to twelve million. This growth was almost entirely the product of immigration, in which the Irish took the lead, followed closely by the Germans, with large groups from southern and eastern Europe coming late in the century. The priority of the Irish, and their aptitude for ecclesiastical organization, gave them a dominant place in the clergy, whose character has been shaped by their combination of businesslike practicality and simple devotion. The immigrant groups generally

[5] One other religious tendency should be mentioned: the vogue of communistic settlements, of which Harmony, Oneida, and Amana are the best known.

tended to congregate in the large urban centers and to find their social place in the industrial working class. For this reason, Roman Catholicism in America has been fairly sympathetic to the workingman, escaping the class bias which cost the Church so much in Europe. The large numbers, rapid increase, and relative poverty of their constituency forced the clergy to devote almost all their energies to the institutional development of the Church—the founding of parishes and the building of churches, schools, and related institutions. This problem was magnified when the American hierarchy decided that it was necessary to organize a separate Catholic school system, since the neutrality of the public schools concealed a subtle Protestant bias. These tasks strained the resources and occupied the attention of American Catholicism largely to the exclusion of the equally great task of working out a Catholic response to American pluralistic society.

The rapid growth of American Catholicism was marked by a number of internal conflicts. The fact that American law recognized churches only as voluntary associations tempted some of the laity, early in the century, to assert the right of the congregation to control Church property, and this movement of "trusteeism" had to be repressed by the bishops. Conflicts of nationalities were frequent. The Irish at first had to deal with French *emigrés* and missionaries, who supplied most of the early bishops; and after Irish leadership was established it was contested by the Germans, who looked to the Church to preserve their nationality as well as their faith. "Cahenslyism," a movement which sought to organize dioceses by nationality, was defeated by the more normal territorial principle, although some concessions were made to ethnicity at the parish level.[6] The last decade of the century was marked by a conservative reaction against a liberal tendency to exalt American democracy and religious freedom. Cardinal Gibbons, Archbishop Ireland, and Bishop Keane were the spokesmen of this liberal element, which was struck only a glancing blow by Leo XIII's condemnation of "Americanism."

[6] Some of the Poles, feeling that their nationality was neglected, seceded in 1897 and formed a Polish National Catholic Church.

The Church's opposition to the "thesis" of religious freedom was not allowed to interfere with the practical adjustment of American Catholicism to a pluralistic society.

The continual necessity of responding to the needs of successive waves of immigrants delayed the arrival at maturity of American Catholicism. Intense dedication to practical problems precluded the growth of a rich intellectual life, and the poverty of the immigrants prevented Catholics from rising to positions of leadership except in a few specialized areas. Hence the "free Church in a free state" did not produce the expected result of a Catholicism which contributed substantially to the larger community. What it did produce was a flourishing institution which held the faith of the immigrants to an extent which could not be matched in more exclusively "Catholic" countries. The American Church had been the object of missionary concern in its early years; by 1908 it was no longer regarded as a missionary Church, and indeed it was ready to become one of the bulwarks of Catholicism throughout the world. At the price of a certain narrowness of outlook, American Catholicism had succeeded in its basic tasks of reaching and retaining the Catholic immigrants. When massive immigration ceased after 1921, the Catholic population was finally stabilized. American Catholicism reached maturity in the mid-twentieth century, at a time when evangelical Protestantism was losing its position of exclusive leadership and a broader religious consensus of Protestants, Catholics, and Jews was being evolved.

If the American religious achievement is judged by a comparison with nineteenth-century Europe, the verdict must be very favorable to America. Alexis de Tocqueville, a shrewd European observer, asserted that there was "no country in the whole world in which the Christian religion retains a greater influence over the souls of men than in America." American religion had reclaimed to Christianity the bulk of a population which, at the time of independence, seemed to be on the point of lapsing into infidelity. The revival which largely failed in Europe largely succeeded in America. The triumph was all the more impressive because it was accomplished without the artificial support of the state.

American Christianity, however, had set itself a higher objective than that of a simple experiment in voluntaryism. Throughout American history there runs the theme of a special national vocation, the idea that the American people had been set apart by God as "the last, best hope of mankind," chosen to erect on virgin soil a truly Christian nation. This concept of "the kingdom of God in America" can be traced from its first articulation by the Puritans through successive generations of revolutionaries, revivalists, and reformers. In practice this Christian ideal has been regarded as bound up with a more secular ideal, American democracy, which, it must be remembered, was itself based on an assumption of a common morality ultimately of Christian origin. There is something at once noble and pathetic in the "American dream." It has been a continual impetus to reform; in the hands of its greatest spokesmen, such as Lincoln and Wilson, it has raised a common people to the highest levels of national vision. At the same time, the sanctification of democracy has often degenerated, by easy stages, into the justification of whatever results were actually produced by democracy in America. The churches, by the very fact of their independence of the state, were dependent upon the good will of their members, and it has been easier for them to reflect public opinion than to lead it. They have, moreover, tended to idealize the moment of their greatest success, the period of revival in the early nineteenth century, and to seek to perpetuate the individualistic virtues of the growing, self-reliant, and largely rural nation that was America at that time. This desire to perpetuate a lost moment of history is the American counterpart of the European churches' commitment to the ideals of the immediate post-Revolutionary moment of reaction and romanticism. America was uniquely fortunate that the ideal sanctified by its churches was the ideal, not of an upper class, but of the majority of the population.

19

The Mission Field

From a world-wide rather than a European standpoint, the outstanding feature of the religious history of the nineteenth century was the geographical expansion of the Christian faith. For centuries Christianity had been effectively confined to the continent of Europe. The Roman Catholic Church had enjoyed a brilliant period of missionary endeavor in the sixteenth century; but Protestantism remained, except for the British colonies, the peculiar religion of northwest Europe. In the nineteenth century, both Catholics and Protestants took part in missionary enterprises which resulted in the greatest geographical expansion of Christianity since the first ages of the Church, bearing witness to the faith in virtually every part of the globe. K. S. Latourette, the leading historian of the missions, calls this the "Great Century," in which Christianity became truly a world-wide religion. At the same time as the churches were losing much of their base of support in Europe, they were making gains overseas which promised new hope.

The expansion of Christianity was an integral part of the expansion of European civilization in the nineteenth century, the great age of imperialism. European nations established their political domination over the larger part of the world, and their commerce penetrated even where their arms did not. No part of the globe escaped the influence of at least some of the elements of Western civilization. By contrast, the indigenous cultures of the non-Western world were generally in a state of decline, and many were effectively disintegrated by the impact of European civilization. Asia and Africa experienced an extensive cultural shock; and in many areas a spiritual void was created which offered an opportunity for the spread of European ideologies, of which the Christian faith was the most vigorous. Christianity enjoyed the prestige of being a part of the dominant culture, the material support of the vigorous European economy, and the *élan* of a progressive and optimistic society at the height of its power.

Although some governments gave practical assistance to the missions as part of their imperialistic activity, this was an age in which state and Church were separating, and most missionaries were independent both of state support and state control. This freedom was an advantage, since voluntary efforts, stimulated among Catholics by Ultramontanism and among Protestants by evangelicalism, provided greater impetus and wider support for missions, with fewer restrictions, than the state-sponsored efforts of previous centuries. The missionary movement was a part of the general revival of Christianity in the early nineteenth century, whose characteristics it shared. But whereas the revival in Europe came into conflict with the leading secular trends of the age—liberalism, democracy, and scientific thought—these issues were less significant in the mission fields.

The missionaries spread not only the Christian religion but many other elements of Western culture, particularly through their extensive educational establishments. Christianity was merely a part of the bewildering complex of ideas, institutions, and techniques which constituted Western civilization and which was disseminated by the missionaries, whose indirect influence was thus greater than the number of their converts would indicate. Some of the non-Christian religious and ideological movements of the nineteenth and twentieth centuries—the Brahma Samaj and Gandhism in India, Chuntokyo in Korea, the Taiping rebellion and the Kuomintang in China—show the influence of Christian ideals divorced from their theological context. The contribution of the missions to the development of the new nations of the non-Western world was more, perhaps, than they intended or desired.

The missions of the Roman Catholic Church were largely the product of the Ultramontane revival. The autonomous activity of the Papacy, which was able to exercise direct control over most missionary areas through the Congregation *de Propaganda Fide*, was an effective stimulant to action, breaking through the restrictions imposed by the royal patronage of previous centuries. The growth of the religious orders—the new congregations, the revived older groups, and the restored Jesuits—provided a body of priests and nuns for the work of conversion and education. Until the belated emergence of a native clergy, the Roman Catholic missions were dominated by the religious orders. Another outstanding feature was the pre-eminent role of France, which supplied over two-thirds of the missionaries. Paradoxically France, where the Church suffered its most serious reverses in the nineteenth century, was at the same time the source of its greatest missionary effort. This was partly the result of voluntary lay support, organized by the Society for the Propagation of the Faith founded in Lyon in 1822. The French government also lent its assistance, regarding the missionaries as agents of French culture and influence; even the anti-clericals of the Third Republic, who attacked the congregations in France, supported their work abroad. Despite this, the emphasis of the Roman Catholic missions was not on political or cultural influence but on the building of the institutional Church, from mission stations to vicariates-apostolic to the eventual organization of an ordinary hierarchy.

In many areas, the Roman Catholic missions were able to build on the foundations laid by the Portuguese and Spaniards in earlier centuries. Their numbers grew by births as well as by conversions, and Catholics outnumbered Protestants in the mission world. Their influence on the native societies was, however, limited; Catholic missionaries tended to restrict themselves to the development of the Catholic community. The Protestants, latecomers to the mission field, were less numerous, but the growth of their churches was proportionately more rapid. Further, their educational and medical efforts were directed to many who proved insensitive to the Christian faith, so that they exercised a profound, if diffuse, influence on the societies in which they worked. For Protestants, the missions had an additional significance: for the first time Protestantism was able to reach non-Europeans and to become a world religion.

The Protestant missionary movement began, at the end of the eighteenth century, as an outgrowth of the evangelical revival.[1] It was the product of private initiative, and it was characteristically organized in the form of voluntary associations. The pioneer in this movement was William Carey, a Baptist cobbler who, intending to be a missionary in India, obtained the support of a Baptist Missionary Society in 1792. Inspired by this, a group of evangelicals of several denominations, largely under Congregationalist leadership, organized the London Missionary Society (L. M. S.) in 1795. Anglican evangelicals founded the Church Missionary Society (C. M. S.) in 1799.[2] By the end of the decade two Scottish societies had been founded, despite some resistance to missionary work by rationalist elements in the Kirk. The L. M. S. sponsored a missionary society organized in the Netherlands in 1797 and influenced others in Germany, where the Moravians had prepared the way. A number of missionary organizations were founded on the Continent, of which the most famous was the Basel school opened in 1815. Meanwhile an American Board of Foreign Missions had been founded in 1810. Bible and tract societies also joined in the missionary work. The majority of missionaries were supplied by Britain and the United States. British leadership was inevitable, since Britain was the greatest colonial and commercial power. Thus the Protestant missions came to be pervaded by the generalized humanitarianism of British evangelicalism; they promoted education and medicine and sometimes protested against the exploitation of the

[1] There had been some earlier missionary efforts: John Eliot and later the Moravians among the American Indians, and Hans Egede in Greenland.

[2] Two older Anglican societies, still active, were the Society for Promoting Christian Knowledge (S.P.C.K.) and the Society for the Propagation of the Gospel (S.P.G.), founded in 1698 and 1701 under High Anglican auspices.

native peoples. The missionaries worked to complete the destruction of slavery and the slave trade,[3] to prevent the sale of arms and drink to the natives, and to raise the status of women.

While many of the missions were sponsored by specific churches, the necessities of the missionary situation brought about patterns of interdenominational cooperation. Many of the missionary societies were interdenominational; in other cases, the churches agreed to work in separate areas to avoid duplication and confusion. It was soon discovered that the divisions among Christians hindered the work of conversion, and missionaries in the field were quicker than the home churches to realize the necessity of union. One form which this took, in the latter part of the century, was the "faith mission," the work of individuals without the support of any organization, motivated only by their own inner dynamic. The China Inland Mission was the type of this mission, which proved especially appealing to American evangelicals. As native churches began to be organized, they proved unusually ready for ecumenism, forming interdenominational organizations and even achieving some mergers. The missionary movement played a major role in the early stages of Protestant ecumenism, thereby exerting a significant influence on Europe itself.

In India, the first country reached by the evangelical missions, an extensive Roman Catholic missionary effort had already been commenced by the Portuguese in the sixteenth century.[4] These missions declined as Portuguese power waned, but Portugal still claimed ecclesiastical supremacy (*real padroado*) over all Indian Catholics. This claim was rendered absurd by the growth of Brit-

---

[3] Incidental to this was the founding, under evangelical leadership, of Sierra Leone and Liberia as colonies for freed slaves.

[4] Syrian Christians (so-called Christians of St. Thomas) were in India before the coming of the missionaries. Some of them were monophysites (Jacobites) and others were Roman Catholic Uniates. The latter received bishops of their own under Leo XIII. Some of the former, invigorated by evangelical contacts, formed the Mar Thoma Church, which was in communion with the Anglicans.

ish power, which by the mid-nineteenth century had been extended over the entire sub-continent, and by the coming of British Catholic missionaries. Rome felt free to disregard Portuguese
pretensions, dividing India into vicariates-apostolic in 1832. The
Portuguese clergy, refusing to submit, brought about a schism
which lasted until 1886, when a partial compromise was reached
which allowed a hierarchy to be formed. Despite the schism, the
numbers of Catholics grew rapidly throughout the century; most
of the increase was by births, but many converts were made,
usually in groups, among the lower castes and primitive tribes.
Native Indians were used as catechists, and eventually the native
clergy outnumbered the missionaries.

Protestant missionary work had begun in 1706 with German
pietists supported by English funds; but the British East India
Company, which governed the British possessions, hindered missionary efforts which, it was felt, interfered with commercial relations with the natives. The first Anglican chaplains were sent out
in 1793. That year was also notable for the arrival of the Baptist
William Carey, who was the real founder of the Protestant missions and was responsible for translating the Bible into several
Indian languages. When the charter of the East India Company
was renewed in 1813, freedom of action was permitted to missionaries, and the Anglicans erected a bishopric. After the crushing of the Indian Mutiny and the assumption of direct government by the British Crown in 1858, the Protestant missions grew
rapidly. By 1914 Indian Protestants numbered one million,
which was half the number of the Roman Catholics but represented a more rapid expansion. Most of the converts came from
the out-castes and tribes. The development of a native clergy was
promoted and, in 1912, the first Indian (V. S. Azariah) was elevated to the Anglican episcopate. The most significant work of
the Protestant missions was in education, where they contributed
to the growth of an English-style educational system which was a
major factor in the Westernization of India. In this regard their
work had effects far beyond the limited circles of Indian Christianity, which represented only one per cent of the total population.

Large numbers of Protestants in the Orient were found in two
countries whose Christian history was largely shaped by the

Dutch. Ceylon, originally a Portuguese possession, was conquered by the Dutch in the seventeenth century; several hundred thousand natives were converted to Protestantism, largely by compulsion. After the British took over the island in 1801, the Dutch Protestants declined in numbers, and the Roman Catholics regained their strength. Later British Protestant missionaries arrived. By the beginning of the twentieth century Christians numbered about one-tenth of the population, an unusually large percentage. The other area of Dutch influence was the East Indian islands (now Indonesia), where the Dutch East India Company had both supported and restricted the Reformed Church. Late in the nineteenth century, when Kuyper came to power in Holland, the "ethical policy" was adopted which required the state to further the welfare of the natives and also to encourage the missions. Although the Moslems, the bulk of the population, were largely impervious to the appeal of Christianity, thousands of converts were made from the animistic tribes.

Except for the Philippines, converted and ruled by the Spanish since the sixteenth century, the largest number of Roman Catholics in Asia was to be found in the area known as Indo-China. French missionaries had begun making converts in the seventeenth and eighteenth centuries, and military intervention in support of the missionaries gave France its first territorial conquests in the area. After a succession of persecutions and interventions, Indo-China came under complete French control by 1884. The missionaries drew every advantage from the French conquest. By 1914 there were nearly a million Catholics.

The greatest of the mission fields was China, with an immense population, an ancient civilization, and an empire which was destined to be rudely shaken by the impact of the West in the nineteenth century. Christianity had been brought to China, after earlier contacts had left no lasting result, by Jesuit missionaries in the sixteenth and seventeenth centuries. The Jesuits made a remarkable attempt to synthesize Christianity and Confucianism, but they were hampered by their fellow Catholics, who objected to too much accommodation to Chinese culture in the matter of reverence for ancestors. Eventually the imperial government stiffened its attitude and persecuted the Christians.

The reopening of China to Christianity was a by-product of the Opium Wars of 1839–42 and 1856–60, in which the Chinese were completely defeated by Western armaments. Britain and France imposed terms which included the opening of several ports to European trade and residence, extra-territorial status for foreigners, and freedom for missionary activities. Resentment against foreigners, which extended to the missions, burst out on several occasions, notably the Boxer uprising in 1900; but this was crushed by European intervention, and thereafter Chinese resistance to Westernization weakened. Some of the bulwarks of the old culture collapsed when the Confucian examination system was abolished in 1905 and the empire was replaced by a republic in 1911.

In China, the Roman Catholics made the most converts and the Protestants exercised the largest influence on the nation. The Catholics, building on earlier foundations, devoted their attention largely to the growth of the Church, which embraced over a million Chinese by the end of the century. The first Protestant missionary, Robert Morrison, arrived in 1807; but extensive Protestant work could only begin after the Opium Wars, particularly after the opening of the interior in 1860. The growth was rapid, many denominations taking part, with the Americans and British supplying the bulk of the missionaries. The largest and most remarkable missionary group was the China Inland Mission, founded by James Hudson Taylor in 1865. This was a "faith mission," whose workers went forth without organized support in the trust that "the Lord will provide." Another feature of the Protestant missions was the emphasis on education, particularly secondary and higher education. Their universities were the leading institutions for the importation of Western ideas into China, thereby contributing to a process of Westernization which extended far beyond the community of Chinese Protestants, who numbered perhaps half a million. Significantly, Protestants provided an extremely large proportion of the leaders of the republic founded in 1911.[5]

[5] In view of the subsequent triumph of Communism, the identification of Protestantism with the Kuomintang regime was a somewhat equivocal success.

Korea, a dependency of China, persecuted Roman Catholic missionaries and converts until the 1880's. In that decade extensive Protestant missions began, largely American in origin and eventually outnumbering the Catholics. Some one per cent of the population was converted, more than in China or Japan, and an extensive educational work was begun, although Western Christian influence was somewhat counteracted after 1910 by the Japanese annexation of Korea.

Japan, like China, had been reached by Jesuit missionaries in the sixteenth century; but an intense nationalistic reaction not only crushed the missions [6] but isolated Japan from Western contacts until it was "opened," under the threat of superior armaments, after 1854. The Japanese response to the technological supremacy of the West was unique; while retaining their loyalty to ancient traditions, they reorganized their government, economy, and education, adopting the most approved European models so successfully that, by 1895, they were able to join the European imperialists in the exploitation of China. The adjustment of Japan to the outward elements of Western civilization, which saved it from Western political domination, also allowed the subtler elements of Japanese culture, particularly its religious traditions, to continue in stability. Nonetheless, Christian missions were able to make some penetrations in Japan. Between 1858 and 1873, under Western pressure, the persecution of Christianity ceased and missionaries were allowed to enter. French missionaries brought Roman Catholicism; Russian Orthodoxy scored its only successes outside Siberia and Alaska; but the Protestants made the largest number of converts—about one hundred thousand. Their impact on society was less than elsewhere, largely because the state, while maintaining the old Buddhist and Shinto religions, undertook the task of Westernization, particularly in education, which would otherwise have fallen to the missions.

One feature is common to all the missions to the Orient. They were able to win relatively few converts among the dominant

[6] A tiny remnant of Japanese Christians survived in obscurity, although their Christianity was much corrupted. Some of them eventually rejoined the Roman Catholic Church.

groups of the civilized populations: Moslems, upper-caste
Hindus, Buddhists, Confucians, and Shintoists. Their successes
came chiefly among the depressed classes and animistic tribes, the
latter usually converted in groups. While the cultural impact of
the West on Asia, to which the missionaries contributed, was
great, the number of Asian Christians was, except in some local
areas, insignificant in proportion to the population. The resistance of Islam to Christianity was striking; indeed, it is likely that
Moslems have made as many converts as Christians in the last
century. In heavily Moslem areas such as the Near and Middle
East, Western Christianity achieved few conversions. The extensive mission effort to the Near East, in fact, devoted itself almost
exclusively to the existing communities of Oriental Christians,
reviving, and sometimes changing, their faith. In general the
areas of higher culture were less receptive to Christianity than
the more primitive cultures. The greatest proportionate successes
of the Christian missions were won among less advanced societies
than those of Asia. On many of the islands of the Pacific (Tahiti,
Fiji, Tonga, and Hawaii) the bulk of the native populations
were converted. The most promising field of missionary endeavor, however, was the "dark continent" of Africa.

Africa had been known to the West chiefly as a source of slaves,
and European influence had been confined to coastal posts. The
nineteenth century was the great age of exploration, followed
rapidly by partition among the European powers, so that by the
end of the century all the continent, except Liberia and Ethiopia,[7] was under European political domination. One of the
greatest explorers of the interior was a missionary, David Living-
stone, whose work drew much attention to the area; and among
the excuses for the extension of European control was protection
of the missionaries and suppression of the slave trade. The partition of Africa left Britain and France as the leading colonial
powers, and these two nations also took the lead in missionary
work. The impact of Western culture was a shock to the primitive African societies, and much of their culture disintegrated.
This provided an opportunity for Christian missions to fill the

[7] Ethiopia had an indigenous form of Coptic Christianity.

cultural void; indeed, the missions represented the best effort of Europe to repair the destruction it had wrought. The Protestant missions, working up from South Africa, were most successful south of the Zambezi. The Roman Catholic missions started from Algeria, conquered by the French in 1830, where Cardinal Lavigerie organized the "White Fathers" to work among both Moslems and pagans. Their greatest successes were scored south of the Sahara. The Belgian Congo was, after 1884, another great area of Roman Catholic activity. By 1914, Protestants and Roman Catholics each had over a million members in Black Africa. Their work was complicated by the competition of Islam and by rivalries among the colonial powers.[8] Perhaps nowhere else were the missions so intimately involved in the total imperial enterprise of the European nations. This undoubtedly facilitated the task of the missionaries in the nineteenth century, but it rendered the missions vulnerable to African resentment when the age of imperialism came to an end.

Was the nineteenth century indeed the "Great Century" of Christian expansion? Latourette, in 1950, had no difficulty in so describing it. Although the proportion of Christians to the total population of Asia and Africa was very slight, their numbers grew rapidly in nearly every country, and the early twentieth century promised still greater expansion. The slowness of the churches to develop a native clergy[9] was eventually overcome, and the "Younger Churches" were becoming self-reliant and taking a larger part in the affairs of Christendom. It might well appear that Christianity was making gains in the new nations which outweighed the losses it had suffered in Europe.

It is no longer possible to make so sanguine an estimate. The situation has been radically altered by the rise of nationalism

[8] The extreme instance of this was in Uganda, where a three-cornered civil war was waged by the supporters of the Arabs (Moslems), French (Roman Catholics), and British (Protestants).

[9] The development of the Roman Catholic clergy was necessarily hindered by the requirement of learning Latin; but in some areas there was also a tendency to limit the native priesthood to the higher castes.

and the elimination of the colonial empires in Africa and Asia. From the Afro-Asian standpoint, the missions had been merely the religious aspect of Western imperialism; and the native churches were as yet too young to have lived down their foreign origins. The "secular religions" of Communism and nationalism had greater appeal in the underdeveloped countries than Christianity.[10] Independence has proved a painful fact to the "Younger Churches." The destruction of the Chinese missions can no longer be considered merely a temporary interruption; and the superficiality of many conversions has been revealed in parts of Africa. To be sure, the "Younger Churches" may adjust to the new situation, aided by the ecumenical movement and the development of native liturgies. But it is clear that Christianity is not growing as rapidly as rival faiths, both religious and secular. As the "population explosion," which in the nineteenth century increased the strength of Europe, works its effects in Asia and Africa, the Christian proportion of the world's population will decline.

At this date it would be premature to assess the ultimate achievement of the missions. Perhaps, when such an assessment can be made, it will be done not by historians but by anthropologists. The bringing of European Christianity to the non-European world was, after all, an immense experiment in inter-cultural relations. The early missionaries were largely unaware of this dimension of their work. With a few (mostly Roman Catholic) exceptions, they had little respect for native culture, were confident of the superiority of the West, and were filled with that sense of the righteousness of their mission which was necessary for a successful apostolate but may have been a trifle annoying to the objects of their concern. It was fortunate for the nineteenth-century missionaries that they worked at a unique moment in history, when the strength of Europe was at its highest point. They were worthy of that moment of opportunity; but they could not perpetuate it.

10 Marx was wrong: Christianity was not the "opiate of the people," if only because it reached so few of them. The real "opiate of the people" has been nationalism.

20

The Century of Missed Opportunities

The nineteenth century was the century of missed opportunities. It was a period of religious revival, of great expansion of Christian activity, outreach, and accomplishment. It was also a period in which, viewed in relation to the society in which they worked, the Christian churches failed to make the impression or achieve the results warranted by this outpouring of zeal and energy. The disproportion between the extent of the revival and its limited effects on European society is the central problem of nineteenth-century religious history.

How did this paradoxical situation come about? Part of the explanation is to be found in the circumstances external to religion: the novelty of the problems to which the churches were required to find answers, and the strength of the forces hostile to Christianity in an age in which many of the old bulwarks of religion were shattered. Part of the answer may be found in the quantitative aspects of the problem, in the immensity of the challenges presented by a constantly expanding society; so much of the energy of the churches was exhausted in the effort to keep up with the rapid growth and movement of the population. Yet these are only partial answers, for challenges are also opportunities. Much of the relative failure of the Christian revival must be attributed to a failure within the churches themselves to rise to the opportunities presented by the "Great Century."

The seeds of this failure are to be found in the very elements

223

which were responsible for the revival of religion. That revival was an inseparable part of the reaction against the Enlightenment and the Revolution, a reaction which was to prove but a temporary pause in a century of change. The political aspects of this reaction were especially unfortunate. The French Revolution, however harshly it had dealt with the churches, had also cleared the ground, liberating religion from its traditional dependence on the state and its stifling entanglement with secular society. The churches, however, sought to return to the deadly embrace of a dying world; freed from the states, they developed new ties to the social order. This meant a rejection of the liberal and democratic movements which were not merely destined to dominate the century but which represented its most generous secular aspirations.

The intellectual consequences of the linkage of revival with reaction were more subtle. Religion was associated with the peculiar thought-forms of the Romantic era and especially with its anti-intellectualism. Evangelicalism, with its emphasis on emotional experience, and the Roman Catholic revival, with its medievalism and reliance on authority, met the needs of the immediate post-Revolutionary situation but left the churches unprepared for the renewed surges of intellectual inquiry later in the century. The arguments which might refute Voltaire were not sufficient against Huxley; and those within the churches who sought to construct new apologetics found their integralist co-religionists more difficult to deal with than their secularist opponents.

The intellectual challenges were most powerfully felt in Protestantism, the political in Roman Catholicism. Both suffered from the growing alienation of the masses of the population, for the outlook of all churches was still bound to a socio-economic order which was doomed by the industrial as well as the political revolution. Thus the factors which made the early nineteenth century so great a moment of religious revival worked to limit the future successes which might be won by churches which vainly sought to perpetuate that moment.

The association of revival with reaction meant also the rejection of the unique opportunities afforded by the post-Revolutionary situation of Europe. For the first time, perhaps, since its establishment by Constantine, Christianity was free to develop in independence of the existing political and social order. The Christian religion had not always been a conservative force; and in the new freedom of the nineteenth century it had as great an opportunity as any of the new revolutionary movements—provided the churches were willing to accept the risks of the free competition of ideologies. That they did not do so is the substance of this narrative; that they could have done so gives point to this narrative. Throughout the century the churches consistently chose the easiest course, relying upon the broken reeds of states, classes, and traditions rather than upon the naked strength of the faith itself. This was the ultimate betrayal—a betrayal of self. It is a significant judgment upon nineteenth-century Christianity that its most stiking successes were won outside the protected confines of Europe, in the open atmosphere of the new nations and the missions. In the twentieth century the center of the Christian world has moved from Europe, if not all the way to America, at least to the thirtieth degree of longitude; and it is fashionable to speak of European society as "post-Christian."

We should not judge too harshly. If this was a century of missed opportunities and outward losses, it was also an age of internal growth in which the churches matured in discipline and devotion and many individuals found genuine spiritual satisfaction in their religion. The religious revival failed because of what was best, not worst, in it. It had stirred up moral strivings which could not be satisfied within the institutional framework of nineteenth-century Christianity. The revival and intensification of the faith went hand in hand with its growing isolation from the larger trends of European society. The Church militant won its triumphs, but it did not succeed in transforming itself into the Church relevant. That task remained, under more difficult circumstances, for the twentieth century.

Recommended Books for
Further Reading

This is an introductory guide to assist the reader who wishes to pursue further the study of particular phases of modern church history. More detailed bibliographies may be found in such works as Latourette, Nichols, Vidler, Hales, and Smith and Jamison (see below).

GENERAL

Burrell, Sidney A., ed. THE ROLE OF RELIGION IN MODERN EURO-PEAN HISTORY. Macmillan paperback. New York, 1964. *A collection of articles by various authors.*

Latourette, Kenneth Scott. CHRISTIANITY IN A REVOLUTIONARY AGE. Vols. I–III. New York, 1958. *A monumental and detailed survey.*

Nichols, James Hastings. HISTORY OF CHRISTIANITY, 1650–1950. New York, 1956. *A textbook with an evangelical Protestant bias.*

Vidler, Alec R. THE CHURCH IN AN AGE OF REVOLUTION. Penguin paperback. Baltimore, 1962. *The English counterpart to this work, with emphasis on British history.*

ROMAN CATHOLICISM

Altholz, Josef L. THE LIBERAL CATHOLIC MOVEMENT IN ENGLAND. London, 1962.

Aubert, Roger. LE PONTIFICAT DE PIE IX (1846–1878). Paris, 1952. *The finest Catholic scholarship in the field. Not available in translation.*

Bouyer, Louis. NEWMAN. Translated by J. Lewis May. Meridian paperback. Cleveland, 1960. *Probably the best of a host of biographies.*

Dansette, Adrien. RELIGIOUS HISTORY OF MODERN FRANCE. 2 vols. Freiburg, 1961.

Fremantle, Anne, ed. THE PAPAL ENCYCLICALS IN THEIR HISTORICAL CONTEXT. Mentor paperback. New York, 1956. *A convenient collection of documents.*

Hales, E. E. Y. THE CATHOLIC CHURCH IN THE MODERN WORLD. Image paperback. Garden City, N. Y., 1960.

——. PIO NONO. London, 1954.

——. REVOLUTION AND PAPACY, 1769–1846. London, 1960. *Provocative revisions by the ablest Catholic historical apologist.*

Vidler, Alec R. PROPHECY AND PAPACY. London, 1959. *A study of Lamennais.*

——. THE MODERNIST MOVEMENT IN THE ROMAN CHURCH. Cambridge, 1934.

PROTESTANTISM

Faber, Geoffrey. OXFORD APOSTLES. Penguin paperback. London, 1954. *Refreshingly free from the odor of sanctity.*

Halévy, Elie. A HISTORY OF THE ENGLISH PEOPLE IN THE NINETEENTH CENTURY. 6 vols. Translated by E. I. Watkin and D. A. Barker. Barnes and Noble paperback. New York, 1961. *See Vol. I, part 3, and Vol. IV, chapter 7.*

Mackintosh, Hugh Ross. TYPES OF MODERN THEOLOGY. New York, 1937.

Meacham, Standish. "The Evangelical Inheritance," JOURNAL OF BRITISH STUDIES, III (November, 1963), 88–104.

Moore, Edward Caldwell. AN OUTLINE OF CHRISTIAN THOUGHT SINCE KANT. London, 1909.

Murphy, Howard R. "The Ethical Revolt against Christian Orthodoxy in Early Victorian England," AMERICAN HISTORICAL REVIEW, LX (July 1955), 800–817.

AMERICA, THE MISSIONS, AND ECUMENISM

Latourette, Kenneth Scott. A HISTORY OF THE EXPANSION OF CHRISTIANITY. Vols. IV–VI. New York, 1941–1944.

Littell, Franklin Hamlin. FROM STATE CHURCH TO PLURALISM. Anchor paperback. New York, 1962. *An independent Protestant interpretation of American church history.*

Mead, Sidney. THE LIVELY EXPERIMENT. New York, 1963. *Essays on American religious history.*

Rouse, Ruth, and Stephen Neill. A HISTORY OF THE ECUMENICAL MOVEMENT 1517–1948. London, 1954.

Smith, James Ward, and A. Leland Jamison, eds. RELIGION IN AMERICAN LIFE. Vol. I. Princeton, 1961. *A collection of essays. Vol. IV is an exhaustive bibliography.*

Ware, Timothy. THE ORTHODOX CHURCH. Penguin paperback. Baltimore, 1963.

Index

Absolutism, monarchical, 47f.

Acton, Sir John, Lord (1834–1902), 77, 82, 84, 161

Acts of 1836 and 1837, 94

Adventists, 203, 205

Aeterni Patris (1879), encyclical, 148

Africa, Africans, 18, 135, 189, 192-193, 212, 220-222

Agence générale pour la défense de la liberté religieuse, 65f.

Agenda, 110

Aggiornamento, 166

Aglipayan schism, 196*n*.

Agnostic, defined, 131

Alaska, 219

Alexander II, Tsar of Russia (reigned 1855–1881), 178

Alexander III, Tsar of Russia (reigned 1881–1894), 178

Algeria, 221

Alsace, 86f.

Altenstein, Karl Freiherr von Stein zum (1770–1840), 110

Amana, 206*n*.

America, Americans, 22, 23*n*., 25ff., 33, 55, 91, 110, 114, 123, 126, 129-130, 141, 142-143, 152, 162-163, 183*n*., 184, 185-186, 187, 190, 196*n*., 197, 199-209, 214, 219, 225 (*See also* Latin America)

American Bible Society, 185

American Board of Commissioners for Foreign Missions, 185

American Board of Foreign Missions (1810), 214

American Revolution, 33, 190, 200

American Sunday School Union, 185

Americanism, 162-163

Anabaptists, 8

Analogy of Religion (Butler), 13

Anglican Church (*See* England, Church of; Ireland, Anglican Church of)

Anglo-Catholics (*See* England, Church of; High church party; Oxford Movement)

Anhalt, 109

Anthropology, 130-131, 222

Anti-drink movement, 141*n*.

Anti-Revolutionary party, 122f.

Anti-Semitism, 143, 150, 155

Anti-trinitarian views, 12

Antonelli, Giacomo Cardinal (1806–1876), 75, 83

Apologia pro vita sua (Newman), 98

Aquinas, St. Thomas (1224?–1274), 148

Arabs (Moslems), 221*n*.

Architecture, 51

Argentina, 196

Arminianism, 8, 27, 204

Arnold, Thomas (1795–1842), 100

Asia, 18, 212, 215-220, 221f. (*See also by country*)

231